Bulletin 63
1950

AREA RESEARCH
Theory and Practice

By

Julian H. Steward

SOCIAL SCIENCE RESEARCH COUNCIL
230 PARK AVENUE   NEW YORK 17

Copyright 1950 by the
Social Science Research Council
Printed in the United States of America

The Social Science Research Council was organized in 1923 and formally incorporated in 1924. Its members are chosen from seven associated professional societies in the social sciences and from related disciplines. It is the purpose of the Council to plan and promote research in the social fields.

ASSOCIATED ORGANIZATIONS

American Anthropological Association

American Economic Association

American Historical Association

American Political Science Association

American Psychological Association

American Sociological Society

American Statistical Association

Committee on World Area Research

Robert B. Hall, *Chairman* — University of Michigan

Ralph L. Beals — University of California at Los Angeles

Wendell C. Bennett — Yale University

W. Norman Brown — University of Pennsylvania

Donald C. McKay — Harvard University

Geroid T. Robinson — Columbia University

George E. Taylor — University of Washington

Staff: Richard H. Heindel

FOREWORD

Area research from the view of the social sciences should, Robert B. Hall proposed nearly four years ago, extend the fund of knowledge respecting the peoples and areas of the world, stimulate interdisciplinary cooperation in research and integration of the findings of research, increase cross-cultural understanding, and provide data and experience tending toward universalization of the social sciences. The task which Julian H. Steward set himself in preparing the present bulletin is essentially that of analyzing the problems encountered in achieving these purposes, although the author more modestly defines what he has done as "an inquiry into some possible scientific concepts, theories, and methods for interdisciplinary area research."

Initiation of an appraisal of techniques of area research was one of five major points in the program of the Council's Committee on World Area Research, outlined at its first meeting in the autumn of 1946. The heterogeneous nature of past attempts at area research and the unorganized character of existing materials, together with the recognition that the impending expansion of programs for training area specialists would rest upon insecure foundations unless these materials could be verified and extended, made it appear imperative that some one attempt to clarify the precise objectives which should guide area research. Definition of the exact scope of the task to be performed and the selection of a competent investigator, however, proved to be exceedingly difficult.

The Committee on World Area Research concentrated its efforts during the next two years on the other four points of its program. A survey of the status of area studies in American universities was completed by Mr. Hall and published in May 1947 as Council Pamphlet 3, *Area Studies: With Special Reference to Their Implications for Research in the Social Sciences.*

In accordance with the Committee's view that special fellowship offerings were essential to strengthen resources for teaching and research, a program of area research training fellowships and travel grants was initiated in the same year. Late in 1947 the Committee sponsored a national conference on the study of world areas which was reported in Council Pamphlet 6, *Area Research and Training,* by Charles Wagley, published in June 1948. A second conference was sponsored by the Committee in May 1950 to review developments in the intervening two and a half years. Some effort was expended too in a preliminary survey of business interests in area training programs.

Meantime the initiation of the appraisal project was again urged in the spring of 1948. It was found that Mr. Steward, as director of a comprehensive project to study the culture of Puerto Rico, had given intensive thought to the problems of area research as a whole. In order that area research workers might have full benefit of his theoretical and practical work, arrangements were made to have him devote part of the year 1948–49 to extending his over-all analysis. A preliminary draft of his manuscript was given critical reading by members of the Committee on World Area Research and others in the autumn of 1949. Final revision of the manuscript was not feasible, however, until the following spring. It is presented here in final form. Its exact objectives are stated in the author's preface.

The appraisal is frankly that of one man, and has been approached, as the author himself states, principally from the point of view of an anthropologist. It is clear that at many points geographers, historians, political scientists, or persons trained in other disciplines would have proceeded with different assumptions and somewhat different objectives. Some area specialists within and outside the Council's Committee question whether any generalized and theoretical definition of area research can span the range of situations from, for example, Puerto Rico to the Soviet Union, which fall within the scope of area research. Nevertheless, many of those who disagree with the author at specific points will agree that he has performed a major service in attempting for the first time to block out a generalized approach in a field notable for the variety and discreteness of the research thus far undertaken. The bulletin should not only challenge further intensive self-analysis on the part of the proponents of other approaches, but may also serve to stimulate individuals competent in other disciplines to attempt their own formulation of the goals which area research should seek to achieve and the techniques which it should use.

PAUL WEBBINK

PREFACE

In the decade before World War II, scientists were seeking ways of compensating for the extreme compartmentalization of knowledge which has characterized twentieth century science. In studies of different world areas social scientists had begun to think in terms of a planned interdisciplinary approach, and a few pioneering projects were undertaken.

In the late 1920's the Carnegie Institution of Washington began a long-range study of the Maya Indians under the direction of Alfred V. Kidder. The problem was to understand Maya culture during all periods from its earliest beginnings to the present day, and the procedure was interdisciplinary in that archaeologists, ethnologists, historians, geographers, biologists, nutritionists, medical research workers, and other specialists participated in the research. The results have not yet been integrated. During the early years of the New Deal several interdisciplinary studies were directed toward the solution of social problems. Under the stimulus of M. L. Wilson, the Soil Conservation Service of the Department of Agriculture enlisted many specialists to study problems of rural resettlement. In cooperation with the Bureau of Indian Affairs, then under John Collier, the Soil Conservation Service sent teams of investigators to study Indian problems in the Southwest and elsewhere. These studies furnished diversified information for administrative purposes, but they were not directly concerned with theory or method. In the late 1930's the Tarascan Indians of Mexico became the subject of a planned scientific interdisciplinary study, which is still being carried on, piece by piece.

With the growing threat of war and a general recognition of the need for greater Hemisphere understanding and solidarity, attention was focused on Latin America. Latin American training centers were created, interdisciplinary research was planned, and the American Council of Learned Societies, National

Research Council, and Social Science Research Council set up a Joint Committee on Latin American Studies which was instrumental in coordinating a great variety of work.[1] A similar approach to other world areas did not receive a strong stimulus until several years later.

Before any coherent theory or method could be developed in area research, the United States found itself in the war. The need for knowledge, not theory, was paramount, and government agencies carried out area research on a large scale. They enlisted the assistance of everyone who had been to foreign areas—scholars, explorers, business men, travelers. Area training programs for the armed services were set up in many universities.

These wartime programs successfully developed interdisciplinary cooperation in that vast amounts of diversified information were processed and interpreted with reference to the immediate problems of how to win the war and how to lay some foundation for peace. Since the war, area programs have been more carefully planned, and there are now area study centers in many universities in the United States.[2] The practical

[1] See *Notes on Latin American Studies*, No. 2 (October 1943).

[2] Area programs have been surveyed and reported on several times. Irving A. Leonard examined the activities of 20 universities in Latin American studies ("A Survey of Personnel and Activities in Latin American Aspects of the Humanities and Social Sciences at Twenty Universities of the United States," *Notes on Latin American Studies*, No. 1, April 1943, pp. 7-46). William N. Fenton discussed area studies in various universities *(Area Studies in American Universities*, Washington: American Council on Education, 1947). Robert B. Hall surveyed the studies in all areas at 24 universities, and described how such studies developed, quoting arguments for and against them, stating objectives, and outlining several programs in detail *(Area Studies: With Special Reference to Their Implications for Research in the Social Sciences*, Social Science Research Council Pamphlet 3, May 1947). Charles Wagley reported on the first national conference on the study of world areas, which was sponsored by the Social Science Research Council's Committee on World Area Research with funds provided by the Carnegie Corporation of New York *(Area Research and Training: A Conference Report on the Study of World Areas*, Social Science Research Council Pamphlet 6, June 1948). This report, like Hall's, deals with general purposes and methods of area studies.

demand that area research supply information to guide our foreign relations is perhaps as great now as it was during the war; but the sense of urgency has diminished sufficiently to enable scholars once again to give thought to the theoretical and methodological implications of their research.

The effort to put area research on a solid scientific basis does not signify a retreat from the rather grim realities of the contemporary world into a realm of pure academic fancy. It means simply that opportunity has come to carry out the fundamental precept that practical needs will be better served by better science. Area research at first tended, especially during the war, to be a catchall proposition in which hundreds of kinds of information were supplied for every conceivable purpose. The principal objective, however, was to understand the nations in foreign areas so thoroughly that we could know what to expect of them, and this required the data of the social sciences and humanities. The problems called for prediction in the field of human behavior. Prediction is also the ultimate goal of purely scientific research, which differs from research carried on for essentially practical purposes mainly in that it can take time to make its assumptions more explicit, to develop its underlying theory, to refine its methods, and to test its hypotheses. As in any field of science, area research may involve speculative theory that is not immediately germane to practical human affairs but in the long run will provide more reliable predictions and sharper analyses of human relations.

The theory of area research poses some difficult problems. The prewar assumption that the data of the social sciences and humanities should be interrelated through an interdisciplinary approach was justified by the success of the wartime programs. An area program serves to integrate knowledge of area phenomena; it is not merely a clearing house for diversified bits of information. But the nature of the area whole has not been adequately conceptualized, and interdisciplinary procedures have not been clarified.

The present bulletin is an inquiry into some possible scientific concepts, theories, and methods for interdisciplinary area research. Current thinking on the theory and practice of area studies has been examined through correspondence, discussion, and some firsthand observation, but the conclusions offered here are the author's own. A survey of area research had been contemplated, but it soon became apparent that it would be premature and presumptuous to make and publish a survey at the present time. In the first place, a great deal of time would have to be spent at each center, discussing problems and research and participating in seminars. In the second place, thinking is progressing so rapidly that it would be unfair and misleading to freeze the ideas of a given moment in print. Finally, the author is doubtful whether he could rid himself sufficiently of his own professionally conditioned thinking to do justice to the ideas of others.

The thoughts expressed in this bulletin have been immeasurably stimulated and sharpened by the thinking of representatives of many disciplines in different area study centers, but they are primarily those of a cultural anthropologist who has had some firsthand experience in area programs. These programs, which will be discussed in more detail in subsequent chapters, include the Latin American research programs which were planned while the author was director of the Institute of Social Anthropology of the Smithsonian Institution, various research programs carried out at Columbia University, particularly the study of Puerto Rican culture, and miscellaneous interdisciplinary and area research projects.

Chapter I of this bulletin examines some of the problems raised by interdisciplinary area research. It reviews the generally accepted objectives of area programs, discusses the concept of area, and states some of the theoretical and practical problems involved in interdisciplinary cooperation.

Chapter II describes some area research which has already been undertaken and which is planned for the future. It was obviously impossible to cover all research that has pertained to world areas, for this would include virtually all social science research. In order to delimit the selection and to place it within some theoretical framework, the unit of study was taken as a first criterion, the units progressing from communities through regions and nations to culture areas. Such units are the basis of most studies that make some pretense of being interdisciplinary and that carry the label of "area research." The many studies of areas made by specialized disciplines might have been reviewed, but such studies have been carried on for years and most of them have no particular bearing on an interdisciplinary approach. A second criterion for choice of illustrations is that the research be concerned with a sharply defined problem, not with description of the area as an end in itself. Such a "problem" could not be the primary criterion for two reasons: first, studies of areas involve a tremendous number of different problems, many of which are in no way interdisciplinary; second, in some studies the problems are very general. An interdisciplinary as contrasted with a multidisciplinary approach, however, makes no sense at all without an underlying interest which dictates the particular problems to be investigated. In Chapter II, therefore, a separate section is devoted to a review of some of the basic themes of interest that pervade all kinds of area research and give rise to a large proportion of particular projects. Even when narrowly disciplinary projects are not brought into clear relationship to one another through any broad statement of problem, theory, or method, they nonetheless tend to relate to central themes of interest, which potentially could be made the basis of an interdisciplinary approach.

Chapter III presents the author's conceptualization of an interdisciplinary area study. Because there is no special *area discipline,* an area approach must spring from special interests, problems, or theories. The concepts and methods presented in this chapter spring largely from anthropology. If these are found to be inadequate, it is hoped that they will stimulate other persons to modify them or to suggest alternatives.

The concepts of Chapter III are illustrated in Chapter IV in a fairly extensive description of the recent project to study the culture of Puerto Rico. While this project is not presented as a model or stereotype for all area studies, it is submitted that the conceptualization of area unit or "whole," which was basic to the project, and such interdisciplinary methods as were attempted in understanding this unit are applicable to other and larger areas. At the same time, the particular problems which oriented the Puerto Rico project arose partly from anthropology, even though their solution required some interdisciplinary collaboration. Had persons from many disciplines participated in stating the problems, the project would surely have been greatly enriched.

It is impossible to acknowledge all of the helpful and stimulating ideas received from area research workers, but special gratitude must be expressed to the following individuals whose views, though not directly quoted, have contributed profoundly to the conclusions reached in this volume:

John W. Ashton, Indiana University
Ralph L. Beals, University of California at Los Angeles
Wendell C. Bennett, Yale University
Theodore C. Blegen, University of Minnesota
W. Norman Brown, University of Pennsylvania
Leonard S. Cottrell, Jr., Cornell University
Cora Du Bois, U. S. Department of State
Fred Eggan, University of Chicago
John F. Embree, Yale University
H. H. Fisher, Stanford University
Alrik Gustafson, University of Minnesota
Robert B. Hall, University of Michigan
Pendleton Herring, Social Science Research Council
Ronald Hilton, Stanford University

PREFACE

Preston James, Syracuse University
Felix M. Keesing, Stanford University
Alfred V. Kidder, Carnegie Institution of Washington
Clyde Kluckhohn, Harvard University
Owen Lattimore, Johns Hopkins University
Howard W. Odum, University of North Carolina
Geroid T. Robinson, Columbia University
Harold Shadick, Cornell University
T. Lynn Smith, University of Florida
George E. Taylor, University of Washington
Charles Wagley, Columbia University
Robert Wauchope, Tulane University
Paul Webbink, Social Science Research Council
The late Walter L. Wright, Princeton University

CONTENTS

	Page
Foreword by *Paul Webbink*	vii
Preface	xi

Chapter

I. Introduction ... 1
    Objectives of Area Research ... 1
    Some Definitions ... 6
    Nature of the Area Unit ... 8
    Interdisciplinary Cooperation ... 13

II. Some Practices of Area Research ... 20
    Community Studies ... 20
    Regional Studies ... 54
    National Studies ... 71
    The "Problem" Approach ... 83

III. Some Concepts and Methods of Area Research ... 95
    Integrating Concepts ... 95
    Sociocultural Wholes as Integrative Levels ... 106
    Sociocultural Systems as Research Units ... 114
    Cross-cultural Problems and Methods ... 117

IV. Theory and Practice of an Area Approach: the Puerto Rico Project ... 126
    The Problem and Objectives ... 127
    Background Knowledge for Area Research ... 129
    Field Studies ... 132
    The Insular or Area Whole ... 140
    Implications for Interdisciplinary Area Research ... 147

V. Summary and Conclusions ... 150

Index of Names ... 157

Index of Subjects ... 159

CHAPTER I

INTRODUCTION

The ideal of interdisciplinary area research encounters serious difficulties in the traditional scope, objectives, and methods of the different social sciences. Anthropology has dealt primarily with primitive peoples and it uses the concept of culture and a comparative method to study the total way of life of tribal societies. No single discipline has attempted the same for civilized societies, whose different aspects are the separate concern of many specialists. Economics, sociology, and political science have concentrated their efforts mainly on Euro-American nations and have paid other world areas comparatively little attention. Geography, language, and the humanities have had long experience in foreign areas, but they too deal with specialized subject matter. Some areas like China early became the specialty of persons who were more interested in history than in contemporary phenomena.

To coordinate the efforts of all these disciplines in foreign area research would require mutual understanding on many fundamental points. First, it would be necessary to obtain agreement on the general objectives of area programs, which determine the selection of specific problems and research methods. Second, there would have to be some generally accepted concept of "area" which would make it more than the "sum of the parts" or features in which the disciplines have traditionally been interested. Third, methods would have to be devised to facilitate interdisciplinary research and to integrate its results. These three problems are considered in the following sections.

OBJECTIVES OF AREA RESEARCH

As far as can be determined there is now general agreement on the following four objectives of area research:

(1) To provide knowledge of practical value about important world areas;

(2) To give students and scholars an awareness of cultural relativity;

(3) To provide understanding of social and cultural wholes as they exist in areas;

(4) To further the development of a universal social science. All four goals carry the implication that an area can be understood only through the cooperation of several disciplines. The last three carry the implication that area "wholes" cannot be understood unless relevant knowledge of social science phenomena is integrated, and consequently they raise the question of the nature of that integration.

To accumulate and make available a body of knowledge of practical utility regarding the principal areas of the world could require investigations of every conceivable kind. During the war there was an enormous demand for hundreds of different kinds of spot information. So far as this demand is concerned, it can undoubtedly be expected that any area specialist will make available whatever miscellaneous knowledge he happens to possess when it is needed. It is not conceivable, however, that one could predict the many kinds of physical, biological, social, and cultural knowledge that will be needed in the future, let alone devise and finance a research program that could gather all such knowledge. Research in any field of investigation has always had to choose from among many possible subjects.

Area research programs are striving to achieve some central purpose, but they cannot cover everything. They cannot even give proportionate attention to the many prevalent scientific and practical interests. Structural geology, foreign trade, military geography, economic potentials, prehistoric fauna, political ideologies, and social classes, for example, may all present legitimate area problems, but these and all other phenomena having area distinctiveness can scarcely be included in an area research

INTRODUCTION 3

program. As a matter of practical procedure, area studies now center attention on the social sciences and humanities, and this is probably because international affairs have acquired such overwhelming importance since World War II that emphasis has to be placed on human relations.

Curricular offerings and research projects reveal recurrent themes in area studies: the development of political ideologies, such as communism, pan-Slavism, pan-Islamism, and national independence movements; colonialism; natural resources, economic potentials, industrialization, and trade; war potentials; changes in backward societies under the influence of industrialized ones; and many others.

In practice these themes of general interest underlie the principal problems selected for research in area programs, and they require a range of knowledge that cuts across the different disciplines. For example, programs of Russian research pay considerable attention to the theme of Russia's international relations. The problem of Russia's relations with the United States alone is the subject of many particular studies made in different disciplines. In the program of the Russian Institute at Columbia University, for example, United States – Soviet relationships are the theme of various publications, essays, and research reports that appear under different headings: under *international relations,* "The Root Mission to Russia . . . ," "United States Decision To Intervene in Russia, July, 1918 . . . ," "Russia, America, and the Armenian Problem, 1918–21," "Izvestia Looks Inside U.S.A.," "America Through Soviet Eyes," and "U.S. Policy and the U.S.S.R."; under *political institutions,* "The United States and the Soviet Union"; and under *literature,* "American – Russian Literary Relations," "Soviet Criticism of Six American Authors," and "Soviet Criticism of Western European Literature." These seem almost to constitute a single, broad project on U.S. – U.S.S.R. relations, and many projects under economics and history also concern U.S.S.R. foreign policy. Other themes of major interest that cut across disciplinary lines are the development of Soviet economics, the growth of political ideology, and treatment of internal ethnic groups.

A great deal of miscellaneous information is pertinent to these basic themes. Most research projects in the social sciences, the humanities, and linguistics so clearly pertain to certain central themes that they could be listed under these rather than under the disciplines involved. This suggests that the themes could provide a basis for interdisciplinary cooperation.

A deepened recognition of cultural relativity means that one knows enough about foreign cultures to understand that each has a self-consistent and distinctive pattern, that each has developed its own solutions to life out of a unique past, and that none is absolute or inherently superior to the others. Such understanding gives the layman greater tolerance of peoples of other areas, and it gives the scholar an objectivity which will help him avoid the methodological fallacy of ethnocentrism, that is, of using the presuppositions of his own culture in dealing with other cultures.

An understanding of social and cultural wholes as they exist in areas is a third object. The concept that each area is organized as a whole is a necessary corollary of the concept of cultural relativity. When cultures of different areas are viewed relatively, each is necessarily recognized as an entity which differs from our own culture in its entirety as well as in many of its particulars. Any one who becomes familiar with a new and different culture experiences what has been called a "cultural shock"—an awareness that everything about the new culture is somehow unfamiliar but also part of a self-consistent and intelligible whole. In attempting to understand a foreign area he finds that to compartmentalize knowledge among the highly specialized disciplines, which have become the orthodox means of studying our society and culture and which are sometimes regarded as evidence of scientific progress, seems somewhat **inadequate.**

Although this specialization is presumed to be valid for study of the United States, where each social scientist participates in the culture and is therefore supposed to be familiar with its basic features, a student of a foreign area finds a need to understand the parts in relation to the whole. "Economic man" does not always strive for profit; "political man" may not know or care about democracy; "social man" may be indifferent to individual freedom; and "religious man" may not at all concern himself with Christian precepts. As knowledge of a foreign area increases, it not only becomes evident that the culture differs from our own in particulars but that these have a consistency or interrelationship that suggests the need for some larger frame of reference for understanding them.

To comprehend social or cultural wholes as they exist in areas an interdisciplinary approach is necessary. The recognition that this is true for foreign areas is even having an effect upon studies of the United States, for a sense of cultural relativity suggests to many scientists who have worked mainly in the United States that our own cultural and social phenomena are relative, not absolute, and that they are interrelated. It has been discovered that the United States is also a "world area" worthy of an interdisciplinary approach, and 16 of the 24 universities surveyed by Hall have programs on the United States.

The objective of *furthering the development of a universal social science* is at present little more than a hope, and an area approach is but one possible means to this end. This objective presupposes, from an area viewpoint, that there are modes of behavior, institutions, patterns, and processes that are universal—that is, which recur cross-culturally or cross-areally. In current thinking, however, there are certain conceptual obstacles to arriving at such universals.

The concept of cultural relativity has often been stated by anthropologists as if all the particulars of behavior patterns and processes differed so completely in each society or area that findings concerning any one society were valid for it alone.

Some economists, sociologists, and political scientists, on the other hand, have assumed that human beings are so fundamentally the same everywhere that rules of behavior which obtain in any one society—for example, our own, which has been the principal object of their investigations—will hold for all other societies so that a cross-cultural approach is scarcely necessary.

If the problem of developing a universal social science is adequately phrased, this seeming contradiction can be resolved. Cultures, societies, and areas have distinctive traditions or histories and unique patterns, no two being alike in their totality. At the same time, it is possible to identify certain institutions and modes of behavior which are similar in different areas. For example, it is true that economic behavior in China or Bali cannot be wholly understood without reference to family structure, religious concepts, and other factors of the total culture. Nevertheless, although the presuppositions about economic man that American economists have acquired through observations of our own culture may not hold for foreign areas, Chinese or Balinese may react in the same way under like circumstances, for example, under a plantation economy. The problem, then, is one of specifying the particular conditions under which similar behavior patterns may be produced.

We shall return to this problem subsequently, for a cross-cultural approach to regularities of human behavior is potentially one of the most fruitful in social science. It is noted here to suggest that the goal of ascertaining universals in social science requires a definite theory and method and that, because behavior of special kinds must be understood in context as well as in isolation, the knowledge and techniques of various disciplines must be brought to bear upon these problems.

Some Definitions

The general objectives just mentioned as well as the practices of current area programs embrace so wide a range of particular

INTRODUCTION

purposes and procedures that it would only perpetuate confusion to discuss them all in the same terms. Some definitions are needed.

Area study and *area program* are very inclusive terms, and *area* has several meanings. It may mean a *world area,* that is, an area of world importance (importance to the United States in its international relations), such as Russia, the Far East, South Asia, or Eastern Europe; it may mean a *culture area,* such as Latin America, the Near East, Middle America, or the Maya Indians, which may or may not have contemporary importance to the United States; it may be a *nation,* such as China, Russia or Brazil; it may be a *colony,* such as the European colonies in Africa; it may be a *dependency,* such as the United States dependency of Puerto Rico; or it may be a *region,* such as the Southeastern United States or the Tarascan Indian area of Mexico. These meanings of *area* are not necessarily mutually exclusive, but each may have distinctive methodological connotations with respect to research.

The term *area program* has a correspondingly wide range of meaning: an undergraduate curriculum; a graduate training program; an interdepartmental seminar; a research program; a single research project. An *area program* may be carried on by a specially endowed and staffed area institute, by interdepartmental cooperation, or by a single department or a single individual.

Because area understanding requires a wide range of knowledge, *interdisciplinary cooperation* is necessary, but this term is meaningless unless the purpose and conditions of the cooperation are specified. In a program of *area training,* which is designed to give a student diversified knowledge about an area, any number and kinds of disciplines may present their offerings. Such a program will be *multidisciplinary* unless the information presented is clearly interrelated with reference to particular problems, in which case it would be *interdisciplinary.* The mere fact that several specialists in different subjects present their information in a single planned curriculum does not necessarily mean that the information is integrated. Some synthesis probably occurs in the mind of the student (the effects of these programs on students would be well worth investigating), and there is much cross-fertilization among the faculty which has attempted to break down disciplinary boundaries through *interdisciplinary* or *interdepartmental* seminars. These seminars frequently undertake some research. In such cases an *interdisciplinary approach* is beginning to appear.

In research, also, distinctions have to be made. An *area research* program may consist merely of several independent research *projects* which are not at all coordinated, or it may constitute a planned *program*. The latter, like a training program, may be *multidisciplinary* in that the several disciplines involved investigate a particular area simultaneously and under a single auspice rather than successively and independently, as used to be the case. It is only collaboration on explicitly defined problems that may make the whole of the specialized research findings larger or more significant than the "sum of the parts."

In most contemporary area study programs, an *interdisciplinary* rather than a *multidisciplinary approach* is considered necessary. An interdisciplinary approach requires an adequate conceptualization of area, of interdisciplinary problems, and of method.

The very need for these definitions suggests that in analyzing the theory and method of interdisciplinary area research, we must examine: (1) the nature of the area unit; (2) the methods of interdisciplinary cooperation; (3) the theory and practice of area research; and (4) the particular problems that guide interdisciplinary study of an area. These are described in this and subsequent chapters.

NATURE OF THE AREA UNIT

In practice, the units selected for area study programs are determined by a number of considerations which may have little to do with scientific theory: the importance of the area in world affairs, the institution's facilities, availability of funds, and others. The natures of the areas consequently differ somewhat.

At the present time there are programs devoted to the following areas: the United States, Middle America, Latin America, Brazil, Western and Central Europe, Scandinavia, Eastern Europe, Russia, the Near East, Africa, South Asia, Southeast Asia, the Far East, China, Japan, Inner Mongolia, and the Pacific Islands. For some of the more important areas, such as Russia, the Far East, and Latin America, there are programs at several institutions. Most of these areas are rather definitely thought of as culture areas in that the nations and societies within each of them have a similar heritage and way of life. Some, like Scandinavia, Brazil, or Western Europe, are cultural subareas; and some, such as Russia, Brazil, the United States, and China, are also nations. Southeast Asia has been described as an "area of political pressures" although it has some cultural and geographic unity.

Cultural, political, and other criteria are not necessarily in conflict. Russia is a subculture of Eastern Europe, while Eastern Europe generally is under political influence from Russia. Cultural and natural areas may also coincide to some degree, or the former may be delimited by such natural features as deserts, mountains, and oceans.

Most of the areas covered in training programs seem rather too large and loose-knit to serve as a frame of reference for all relevant research, and research projects usually have a more limited scope, their area dimensions differing rather considerably according to the nature of the problem. Thus, a geographer might choose to investigate a natural area, such as a river basin, an economist might study a trade area of varying dimensions, and an anthropologist might investigate a community or a region. In contrast to the *primitive culture area*,[1] which was usually quite small and in which a number of fairly independ-

[1] Clark Wissler, *The American Indian* (New York: Oxford University Press, 1922).

ent bands or tribes shared a similar way of life, the *contemporary culture area* or world area not only has a common heritage but the societies or states within it tend increasingly to be linked by economic ties, religious movements, and political ideologies. There is, in other words, increasing functional unity within the area, and to a lesser degree, between areas.

The East European (Finno-Ugric) program at Indiana University is concerned with a marginal area which is characterized by diversity. As a natural area it is marginal to the great East European plains. As a culture area it is intermediate between East and West, sharing features of each and experiencing recurrent strife. It is diversified linguistically, language having become a symbol and carrier of natural, cultural, and political identity.

Russia is the unit of study in several area programs. It is not only culturally part of Eastern Europe, but it is a culture center which, through political, social, and economic forces, is affecting peoples of other cultures.

The Scandinavian area studies jointly sponsored by the Universities of Minnesota and Wisconsin deal with countries which are politically, linguistically, and to some extent geographically and culturally distinctive.

Princeton University's program on the Islamic civilization of the Near East deals with the Moslem peoples from Morocco to Turkestan. The area has cultural uniformity and considerable similarity of environment.

South Asia is defined in the University of Pennsylvania's program as "The nations of India, Pakistan, and Nepal, which together occupy the geographical sub-continent known as India, and the neighboring mountain states of Afghanistan to the northwest and the island of Ceylon at the south." [2] The area has geographical unity, being isolated from other areas, and it has "an inner economic unity, based upon the complementary character and interdependence of the parts," a "unity of politi-

[2] *University of Pennsylvania Bulletin: South Asia Regional Studies Announcement, Academic Year 1949–1950*, p. 4.

INTRODUCTION 11

cal interest, in spite of numerous inner divisions," and a "common cultural heritage." "Nevertheless," it is pointed out, "the delimitation of South Asia in the University of Pennsylvania program might be considered arbitrary in some respects." There is a connection with the Islamic world, and through Buddhism and Hinduism, with Southeast Asia, Central Asia, and even the Far East.

> Besides the religious connections, there have been, and still exist, literary, artistic, and commercial contacts, and even some mutual political interests. . . . There would clearly be logic in delimiting a larger area for an Area Studies program and in treating South Asia in association with the Near East or with Southeast Asia or perhaps with both. The two latter regions might be considered as in the first ring of interest outside the South Asian core. Somewhat further removed, but still associated, would be Central Asia and the Far East. But since a single program covering a wider area than South Asia as now defined would involve certain practical difficulties of staffing and financing, the University of Pennsylvania is at least for the present maintaining the original delimitation.[3]

The Southeast Asia program at Yale University covers the Philippines, Indonesia, Malaya, Burma, Siam, and French Indo-China, an area which is primarily cultural and secondarily geographical. Features common to the area include the growth of nationalism and political regionalism, the early spread of Hindu influence, and many cultural elements such as betel nut chewing. But most training and research programs deal with its cultural subdivisions—Indonesia, Siam – Laos – Cambodia, Vietnam (Annam), etc.—except as problems like the differing effects of Dutch colonialism versus French or British colonialism cut across the cultural subareas and in fact across world areas generally.

The Hispanic American program at Stanford University deals with a very large and general culture area: that portion of America which has a cultural heritage from Spain and

[3] W. Norman Brown, "Area Studies of South Asia," a paper prepared for the session on area studies, Annual Meeting of the Far Eastern Association, April 7, 1949.

Portugal. Outstanding features of this cultural heritage are the use of the Spanish and Portuguese languages, a preoccupation with politics, and the emergence of political figures. The area can be divided into cultural subareas, and it consists of many independent nations. It has geographical unity only in that it occupies a fairly continuous area of the southern portion of the Western Hemisphere.

In the instances just cited, the general area is largely cultural and secondarily geographical. Most of these areas, however, are so large that they must be divided into political units (nations, states, or provinces) or cultural subareas for research purposes. Research projects may have quite different area dimensions, which are determined by the special disciplines involved and by the nature of the research problem.

Ralph Beals' remarks on the program to study the Tarascan Indians of Mexico reveal the difficulty of finding terms of cooperation so long as each discipline conceives its problem and unit of study in traditional ways. He states that an area program may

> "focus on a particular area but the range of investigation will vary . . . from discipline to discipline." . . . In such a study as the Tarascan program, it was soon apparent in planning that while the anthropologist might not go far beyond the boundaries of the habitat of the Tarascan Indians and their neighbors, the studies of other disciplines might have quite different areal definitions. The historian would be concerned not only with this area but also with the state of Michoacan and with the nation of Mexico. The economist would have to consider the state and the nation and be concerned with the general problem of markets and communications in order to study the Tarascans. Areas therefore cannot be rigidly delimited.[4]

The same difficulty of satisfying all disciplines in the definition of an area was encountered at the Middle American Research Institute of Tulane University. The Institute deals

---

[4] Charles Wagley, *Area Research and Training,* Social Science Research Council Pamphlet 6, pp. 14–15.

INTRODUCTION

generally with an environmental-geographical area, but special disciplines or interests might take as their unit of research a modern political area, a geographical entity, a modern cultural unit, a prehistoric cultural unit, a linguistic unit, an area of Indian-Ladino culture clash, or one of Negro-Ladino merging.

Some area specialists have expressed the fear that any attempt to conceptualize an area program too rigidly would force scientists of different disciplines into work that they did not like and could not do well. This idea would seem to rule out any possibility of planned interdisciplinary research.

Where the framework of area research is stipulated in advance by some arbitrarily designated unit, such as a cultural area, political unit, or natural area, the research worker is forced to find a research problem in the subject matter which the area offers. An area, regardless of how it is defined, of course presents a variety of problems that will interest different scientists, but the chances are great that each scientist will focus his attention on a portion of the area which satisfies his own interests and which may not coincide at all with the areas chosen by his associates in other disciplines.

The alternative to finding research problems in prescribed subject matter is to define problems and follow them through whatever areas or subareas are appropriate. This procedure, which is suggested in some of the above programs, is more explicitly advocated at the Walter Hines Page School of International Relations at Johns Hopkins University and in several programs at Stanford University. These are discussed at length in a subsequent section (pp. 83-94 infra).

Interdisciplinary Cooperation

Interdisciplinary Coverage

There is considerable uniformity in the disciplinary coverage of area studies. Differences reflect practical considerations, such as availability of personnel, financial support, and interdepartmental arrangements, more than opinions about ideal coverage. There are certain outstanding lacks in personnel. Economists, sociologists, and political scientists trained in other than Euro-American areas are particularly scarce as are anthropologists trained in study of contemporary civilizations.

While disciplinary coverage may be determined primarily by teaching programs, it affects research in that it tends to prescribe the general scope of operations and the available personnel. Language is always included, for it is not only an essential tool for both practical and scientific work in an area, but it is an important part of the culture. Most of the social sciences and humanities are represented, and there is some discussion of including the medical sciences. The particular subjects included in an area curriculum vary somewhat in undergraduate and graduate programs, and they may differ from one university to another or from one area program to another.[5]

Generally speaking, disciplinary representation in research programs is limited by available personnel. Coverage which exists or is hoped for in some programs is as follows:

Russian program at Harvard University: language, history, anthropology, economics, government, law, social relations, literature.

Russian program at Columbia University: language, history, economics, government, law, international relations, literature, anthropology.

East European program at Indiana University: language, history, economics, government, sociology, anthropology, and folklore.

[5] Hall *(Area Studies,* Social Science Research Council Pamphlet 3, pp. 51–63) describes the various offerings in Latin American studies at Northwestern University, in Far Eastern and in Russian studies at Yale University, in the Far Eastern Department and Far Eastern Institute of the University of Washington, in the China program at Harvard University, and in the Russian Institute at Columbia University. These illustrate different ways of dealing with interdisciplinary and interdepartmental cooperation and with the questions of undergraduate majors and of higher degrees.

European Institute at Columbia University: language, history, government, sociology, economics, public law, literature, fine arts, philosophy, and church history.

Scandinavian program at the Universities of Minnesota and Wisconsin: language, history, economics, political science, sociology, geography, literature.

Southeast Asia program at Yale University: language, political science, sociology, anthropology, geography, international relations.

Pacific-Asiatic, Russian, and Latin American programs at Stanford University: language, history, geography, and humanistic fields.

South Asia program at the University of Pennsylvania: language, history, economics, social institutions and forces, geography, anthropology, demography, religion, philosophy, literature, art, and law; possibly the geological, biological, and medical sciences.

China program at Harvard University: language, history, government, anthropology, humanities, fine arts, literature.

Brazil program at Vanderbilt University: language, anthropology, economics, political science, sociology and, on occasion, many of the physical and natural sciences, especially those dealing with plants, soils, bacteriology, etc.

Japanese program at the University of Michigan: anthropology, economics, fine arts, geography, history, language, literature, political science, sociology, philosophy, social psychology, public health and the more pertinent natural sciences.

Interdisciplinary Integration

Association of scholars as a means of cross-fertilization. At present the principal means of accomplishing an interdisciplinary approach in research as well as in training are joint seminars which are attended by both faculty and students. These are the seedbeds of new research ideas. Hall, writing of the association of scientists of different disciplines as a means of achieving interdisciplinary understanding, concluded: "It seems probable that if a group of social scientists came to know the same limited area well through joint study, they would find much upon which they could agree, partly because of the greater manageability of the data on a limited area and partly because they would have gained better understanding of each other's terminologies and methodologies. A common body of knowledge, upon which all could agree, would form a base upon which cumulative research could be built." [6]

The efforts to effect interdisciplinary cooperation are illustrated by the following:

In the Russian Research Center at Harvard a long-range research program was worked out through a "planning seminar, to which a number of visiting specialists, both British and American, contributed their suggestions. It was agreed to concentrate during the current academic year upon two major projects: a study of the Communist Party in Russia and an investigation of certain topics in the Russian economy." [7] Every project undertaken will attempt to interrelate the approaches of the pertinent disciplines. The studies "have centers of gravity in roughly three areas: politics and history, economics, social relations (anthropology, psychology, and sociology)." [8]

At Minnesota an attempt is being made to integrate the Scandinavian program courses into an "area discipline," as distinguished from the various departmental disciplines, by means of informal discussion among members of the staff and a non-credit course (a kind of proseminar) attended by both faculty and students.

The University of Pennsylvania's South Asia program holds a weekly seminar which is attended by all staff members and

[6] *Ibid.*, p. 49.
[7] Clyde Kluckhohn, "Russian Research at Harvard," *World Politics*, 1:267–272 (1949)
[8] Russian Research Center, Harvard University, "Programs and Census of Current Projects" (mimeographed, January 1949), p. 1.

which takes a major feature of the area as the theme of the seminar for each year. In 1948–49 the subject was "Relations between India and Pakistan"; in 1949–50 it was "An Analysis of Contemporary Political Structure in India and in Pakistan as Affected by Party Organizations, Social Movements, and Religion." In addition to individual research there is coordinated research on the subject of the seminars.[9]

At the Center for Japanese Studies at the University of Michigan, the seminar has settled on two general problems: the impact of industrial civilization upon the pre-Meiji, Inland Sea area; and the effect of the allied occupation program and policy upon this area. These problems will be examined later in other regions of Japan.

Similar seminars are held at other universities. Columbia University's Russian Institute has frequent joint seminars for all staff members and graduate students. Indiana University's East European program has faculty seminars. In the Pacific-Asiatic, Russian, and Latin American programs at Stanford University, interdisciplinary coordination is achieved partly through formal committees but more importantly through informal contacts of the staff. Yale University's Southeast Asia program plans an interdepartmental seminar to include persons from sociology, geography, linguistics, political science, international relations, and perhaps economics.

Integration through research planning and leadership. Some persons believe that integrated area research can be achieved more rapidly and effectively if it is planned and guided by imaginative leadership rather than if it is left to grow out of the exchange of views in joint seminars and research projects. The former procedure would have certain advantages but would also confront certain difficulties.

The fear has been expressed that individuals would oppose what they might regard as excessive regimentation of scholar-

[9] W. Norman Brown, *op. cit.*

ship and even as interference with scientific freedom. This objection seems illusory, for scholars usually take positions because they are interested in doing the particular teaching or research involved. They may refuse a position but, having accepted one, they are rarely free to do whatever their fancies suggest. The problem is one of practice, not principle. It is whether a group of mature scholars, whose training and research have been rather specialized and whose reputations have been established by their particular contributions to knowledge, are emotionally and intellectually able to alter their research habits to an appreciable degree. As long as area centers are staffed with persons who have developed in the tradition of disciplinary research, it is natural that area research should continue to be largely multidisciplinary.

That scholarship can be attracted to planned programs is proved by many of the examples cited in this bulletin. But it is not easy to plan and carry out a truly interdisciplinary program. In the first place, as John F. Embree has observed, leadership must come from some particular discipline, there being as yet no area discipline as such; and it may not be easy to interest other specialists in a program that is unilaterally conceived. The principal exceptions are those programs which have the practical purpose of ascertaining the capabilities and intentions of foreign governments, and even these are under the direction of individuals. In the second place, there are such practical problems as breaking down departmental boundaries, rearranging teaching loads and leaves of absence, and even insuring academic tenure and promotions.

Another consideration is whether a planned approach focused on problems of interdisciplinary interest may not disregard areas per se insofar as area specialists or an area organization are not required. Might it not be possible for a team of investigators to study some particular problem in all parts of the world? There is no doubt that science would profit enormously if problems could be so phrased that similar hypotheses and methods could be used cross-areally and cross-culturally. But research would still have to be carried out in particular locales, and this requires area knowledge.

One of the strongest advocates of an area approach through research on a specific problem is Owen Lattimore, who with his team of workers at the Walter Hines Page School of International Affairs is interested in the postwar development of nationalism. This may be studied as a problem in many areas, the differences between them serving as bases for comparisons. The group at the Page School chose the frontier region between China and Russia for long-term study. This region is part of the much greater Russian-Asiatic frontier stretching from the Black Sea to the Yellow Sea. One of the sample areas selected for study was the Chinese Central Asia Province of Sinkiang,[10] which is inhabited by a mixture of peoples, the overwhelming majority of whom are neither Russian nor Chinese. These people exhibit a number of minority nationalisms, which were examined in relation to many other factors, including geography, economics, communications, and "power politics." Area per se is secondary, and the area chosen—Central or Inner Asia—is really "inter-area," consisting of marginal territories where many influences overlap from the recognized major areas of China, Russia, the Iranian culture-area, and India.

At present most projects that are focused on specific problems tend to be rather restricted in scope, many being essentially unidisciplinary. It is the author's belief, however, that the many themes of interest discussed on pp. 86–94 infra will soon lead to truly interdisciplinary projects, which must be carried out in particular locales, and that these projects can be made to attract specialists from different fields.

[10] Owen Lattimore *et al.*, *Pivot of Asia* (Boston: Little, Brown and Company, 1950).

CHAPTER II

SOME PRACTICES OF AREA RESEARCH

Area research projects that have actually been carried out might be classified in three groups: special disciplinary studies made within particular world areas; studies of entire areas of varying magnitudes; and research dealing with particular problems rather than with areas as such. Studies in the first category present nothing new with respect to areas, and it would serve no purpose to review them here. They are of interest principally as they are related to other studies in terms of a well-defined objective, and when there is such an objective they will be considered under the heading of research on problems. There are many studies which undertake to understand areas as entities, some made largely by a single discipline, some by several disciplines. The areas investigated range from communities through regions, states, and nations to large culture areas. Communities and other smaller units are usually investigated by anthropologists and sociologists; the larger units by representatives of several social sciences. The following sections will consider these studies in order of relative magnitude of the areas concerned. Studies focused on problems are sufficiently distinctive to merit a separate section.

Community Studies

During the past two decades there has appeared a large number of books and monographs which are classed in the broad and rather vague category of "community studies." In the author's opinion, these not only represent anthropology's principal contribution to area research and as such will interest persons of other disciplines, but they also point up some unsolved problems in interdisciplinary cooperation. Detailed analysis of these studies is therefore in order.

The purposes and methods of community studies are extremely varied, but their importance for area research is that they all apply a cultural or ethnographic method to contemporary society. This method was developed by anthropology in the study of primitive peoples, and it is being applied to modern societies by anthropologists and by sociologists who have some knowledge of anthropology. Community studies are still in a pioneering stage, however, and the potential value of the cultural approach to modern society is only incompletely explored. Applied to primitive tribes, this approach has three distinctive methodological aspects. First, it is ethnographic: the culture of a tribe, band, or village is studied in its totality, all forms of behavior being seen as functionally interdependent parts in the context of the whole. Second, it is historical: the culture of each society is traced to its sources in ancestral or antecedent groups or among neighboring peoples. Third, it is comparative: each group is viewed in the perspective of other groups which have different cultures, and problems and methods are used cross-culturally. Two general criticisms may be made of the way in which the ethnographic, historical, and comparative methods are applied to modern communities. First, the methods have not been adapted to modern communities, which differ qualitatively from primitive ones. Second, the historical and comparative methods have been used hardly at all.

(1) The *ethnographic method* has been applied in studies of villages, towns, parts of cities, racial and ethnic minorities, and other special portions or segments of society. Each segment or unit ideally is studied as a whole, the entire range of social science phenomena being covered under such headings as economic life, social structure, political organization, religion, and intellectual activities. In contrast to the more specialized social sciences, which isolate the phenomena they study from their social, cultural, or area contexts, the ethnographic study of a community attempts to integrate all these social science data within the local framework. In this respect a community study

might be considered an interdisciplinary area study in microcosm, except that it is usually made by persons of only one or two disciplines. It is of course far easier to assemble and interrelate all the data of a community than of a nation or other more complex unit.

Most studies, however, have treated the community as if it were a primitive tribe—that is, as if it were a self-contained structural and functional whole which could be understood in terms of itself alone. Scholars are quite aware that any modern community is a functionally dependent part of a much larger whole; but in general they have not yet taken account of this larger frame of reference in community study. Individual communities are often studied as if the larger whole were simply a mosaic of such parts.

For community studies investigators usually select small localized social segments, for these are assumed to constitute cultural subgroups. Though by no means wholly self-contained, these segments are more or less in-groups which have some structural and functional cohesion, and therefore lend themselves to an ethnographic method. It is quite possible that certain occupational groups and classes also constitute sociocultural segments that could profitably be studied by an ethnographic method, but in practice studies of such horizontal segments which cut across nearly all localized segments are more statistical than ethnographic, or are preoccupied with special problems, such as race or class relations.

The ethnographic method is qualitative rather than quantitative. In general, it tends to deal with all the phenomena which are found within a locality. It is open to criticism not because of its lack of quantification but because it treats the local group as if the larger society did not exist. This limitation of the ethnographic method is acknowledged by most investigators of particular communities, who recognize that their studies need to be related to a larger universe of social and cultural phenomena. There are few studies which attempt to show how the larger society affects the community under investigation; and there are no studies which undertake to conceptualize fully and in detail the relationship between the community and the larger whole. Any conceptualization of this relationship will of course depend a great deal upon the problems being investigated. The ethnographic method purports to cover all aspects of community culture, but actually many subjects are omitted because they are best studied in the larger society. It is revealing to compare Wissler's "universal pattern," which is a list of the major subject headings under which all the activities of any group may be described, with the tables of contents of the Lynds' *Middletown* and West's *Plainville*:[1]

Wissler	Lynd	West
Material traits	Getting a living	Technology and economics
Speech	—	—
Art	—	—
Mythology and science	—	—
Religion	Religion	Religion
Family and social system	Making a home	Social structure
Property and exchange	—	—
Government	Community activities (government, health, propaganda, group solidarity)	—
Warfare	—	—
—	Training the young	Life cycle
—	Using leisure	—

The community studies omit such headings as warfare, science, and property and exchange (although the last may be covered in part under other topics). Yet it is perfectly clear that each contemporary community has been very much affected by

[1] Clark Wissler, *Man and Culture* (New York: Thomas Y. Crowell Company, 1923), p. 74; Robert S. and Helen M. Lynd, *Middletown: A Study in Contemporary American Culture* (New York: Harcourt, Brace and Company, 1929); James West (pseudonym), *Plainville, U.S.A.* (New York: Columbia University Press, 1945).

warfare and may be again; that it has been deeply influenced by science as it affects technology, industrialization, and transportation and, through its general invasion of modern life, virtually every other aspect of culture; and that systems of property, inheritance, exchange, and the like are basic to every community although they have dimensions extending far beyond the community. Also, many items in Wissler's "universal pattern" have formal, national aspects that transcend what is found in the community. Most churches, for example, have a formal structure, a doctrine, and an organized authority that are by no means identical with the function and meaning of the church in the community. Some of these universal headings, notably speech, are such familiar parts of one's own culture that one does not even think of including them in a community study in the United States. Yet practically every item in Wissler's "universal pattern," including language and art, are included in area research programs.

It does not follow from this comparison that all the subjects listed should or could be included in all community studies, but it is perfectly clear that these aspects of the larger society do affect the communities and that some procedures are needed to relate them to community phenomena. Some suggestions regarding this problem are offered in Chapter III.

(2) The *historical approach* has been little used in community studies; history is rarely included in them and never covers more than a few years of the immediate past. The result is that analysis of function and process tends to be predominantly synchronic and lacks insights into basic trends that the historical method might give. The difficulties in utilizing more history in a community study are that local historical records are often deficient and the historical problems usually involve the larger society of which the community is a part. Few field workers have the time or patience to do the documentary research that is required. Few even have sufficient interest to interview informants concerning recent history and to use readily available

records to reconstruct changes that have occurred during the past one or two generations.

This comparative indifference to history, in the author's opinion, is a result of the rather uncritical transfer of the methodology of studies of primitive peoples to those of modern societies. A study of a preliterate tribe, which has no recorded history and little traditional history, adds to a body of data which is reconstructed historically by distributional methods and other techniques and which can be used for comparative purposes. It makes a significant contribution to the large field of knowledge about primitive peoples who are little known. But attempts to make functional analyses of culture changes that are now occurring or that have occurred during the period of recorded history are fairly new to persons using the cultural approach. The problems of these culture changes extend far beyond those of a single contemporary community; they involve not only the history of the larger society but require considerable understanding of many specialized subjects. In order to make full use of the historical approach, therefore, problems which are susceptible to research by ethnographic and sociological methods need to be clarified and related to all other disciplines as well as to history.

(3) In a *comparative approach* to contemporary communities, the problems which are studied in one community—or at least the cultural perspectives acquired in any study—are utilized in the investigation of other communities. Ideally, there is some comparability of research projects that have common purposes, problems, and methods. The widely differing characteristics of communities naturally dictate some differences in approach; but individual interests, purposes, and methods have produced even greater differences, and community studies have little in common beyond the fact that they purport to use a cultural method.

It would almost seem that an ethnographic approach and an approach focused on particular problems are irreconcilable. The "pure" ethnographic approach aims to record "imperishable facts" and to avoid theory and problems, while the problem-oriented studies which have been published tend to report data which bear on the problems examined, omitting much ethnographic information. The differences of coverage are so great that it is necessary to consider these monographs in several categories.

One category includes the more purely ethnographic studies, but even these show considerable disparity of emphasis because of varied individual interests. The general chapter headings may be more or less similar, but there is a great difference in purpose and problem. The Lynds' studies of Middletown [2] are concerned with how economic factors and changes affect community life, which is described in most of its aspects. West's *Plainville*,[3] Yang's *Chinese Village*,[4] and Hsu's study of a Chinese community [5] are interested in the interrelation of culture and personality, and following the current approach to this problem, they accord considerable space to the "life cycle"—the development of the individual in the culture. Parsons' Mexican and Ecuadorian studies have the very different purpose of determining the native Indian and Spanish elements in the culture of her communities.[6] Redfield's study of Yucatan, though dealing with folk cultures not unlike those recorded by Parsons, is preoccupied with the transformation of folk societies under urbanizing influences.[7] And Fei's monographs on Chinese

[2] *Op. cit.*, and *Middletown in Transition: A Study in Cultural Conflicts* (New York: Harcourt, Brace and Company, 1937).

[3] *Op. cit.*

[4] Martin C. Yang, *A Chinese Village: Taitou, Shantung Province* (New York: Columbia University Press, 1945).

[5] Francis L. K. Hsu, *Under the Ancestors' Shadow: Chinese Culture and Personality* (New York: Columbia University Press, 1948).

[6] Elsie Clews Parsons, *Mitla: Town of the Souls, and Other Zapoteco-speaking Pueblos of Oaxaca, Mexico;* and *Peguche, Canton of Otavalo, Province of Imbabura, Ecuador: A Study of Andean Indians* (Chicago: University of Chicago Press, 1936; 1945).

[7] Robert Redfield, *The Folk Culture of Yucatan* (Chicago: University of Chicago Press, 1941).

peasants,[8] though reporting on people who are similar to those studied by Yang and Hsu, are concerned with rural economy in its relationship to community types and show no interest in culture and personality.

Other community studies use a cultural approach only in the sense that they endeavor to place the phenomena under investigation in their cultural context. These can hardly be called "ethnographic." In contrast to the essentially ethnographic studies, they constitute a second broad category of social relations studies, which has several subcategories. One subcategory consists of studies of class structure, which became a major interest after publication of the first of the stimulating Yankee City studies by Warner and his colleagues [9] and which is a theme of great interest in studies in several other categories. A second subcategory is concerned with race relations, and it includes a great many studies which deal with the problem of Negro-white relations on a community basis, such as Powdermaker's *After Freedom,* Davis and the Gardners' *Deep South,* Drake and Cayton's *Black Metropolis,* and Dollard's *Caste and Class in a Southern Town.*[10] A third subcategory is social stability studies, such as the Rural Life Studies made by the U. S. Bureau of Agricultural Economics under the direction of Carl C. Taylor.

Differences in emphases of community studies are shown by comparison of the relative amounts of space accorded different subjects in the reports of these studies. The accompanying tabu-

[8] For example, Hsiao-tung Fei and Chih-i Chang, *Earthbound China: A Study of Rural Economy in Yunnan* (Chicago: University of Chicago Press, 1945).

[9] W. Lloyd Warner and Paul S. Lunt, *The Social Life of a Modern Community,* Yankee City Series, Vol. I (New Haven: Yale University Press, 1941).

[10] Hortense Powdermaker, *After Freedom: A Cultural Study in the Deep South* (New York: The Viking Press, 1939); Allison Davis and Burleigh B. and Mary R. Gardner, *Deep South: A Social Anthropological Study of Caste and Class* (Chicago: University of Chicago Press, 1941); St. Clair Drake and Horace R. Cayton, *Black Metropolis: A Study of Negro Life in a Northern City* (New York: Harcourt, Brace and Company, 1945); John Dollard, *Caste and Class in a Southern Town* (New Haven: Yale University Press, 1937).

lation is only approximate, for different authors often discuss the same subject under different headings. The amount of space devoted to a subject depends somewhat, of course, upon its functional importance in the community. Nonetheless, even substantially similar communities are given quite unlike treatment, which reflects individual purposes and methods even more than differences in facts.

Of the essentially ethnographic monographs, Beals' *Cherán*,[11] a study of a village in Mexico, devotes 36 percent of its pages to material culture, economics, and subsistence; whereas Parsons' *Mitla,* also a study in Mexico, allots only 8 percent to these subjects. Hsu's Chinese study (not tabulated) devotes practically the entire volume to the life cycle, Beals' *Cherán* gives it 21 percent of the whole, and Parsons' *Mitla* does not consider it at all. The last study, however, has an illuminating chapter on "town gossip" (20 percent), which contains a variety of informative insights into all aspects of culture. Gillin's *Moche*[12] (Peru) is not very different from *Cherán,* but somewhat fortuitous field circumstances permitted him unusual access to information on curing practices, to which he gives 22 percent of his volume as against 4 percent of Lynd's *Middletown,* while most studies have no such subject heading. Gillin also devotes 10 percent to food preparation, which is of negligible interest in other monographs.

Community studies in the several categories are discussed in the following pages. No attempt has been made to include all monographs that might be classified as community studies nor to cover all conceivable categories, but it is the author's belief that the works mentioned illustrate the principal theories and methods.

[11] Ralph L. Beals, *Cherán: A Sierra Tarascan Village,* Smithsonian Institution, Institute of Social Anthropology Publication No. 2 (1946).
[12] John Gillin, *Moche: A Peruvian Coastal Community*, Smithsonian Institution, Institute of Social Anthropology Publication No. 3 [1947].

PRACTICES

Subject	U.S.A. Middletown	China Peasant*	China Taitou	Japan Suye Mura†	Mexico Cheran	Mexico Tzintzuntzan‡	Mitla	Peru Moche	New Mex. El Cerrito§
History and area	2	5	2	3	4	⎱11⎰	5	8	15
Objective	1	3	0	1	2		0	0	0
Technology, economics, subsistence	14	63	25	22	36	48	8	33	25
Social and political	⎱23⎰	13	48	18	13	4	20	20	50
Life cycle	17	0	0	13	21	14	0	4	0
Religion	17	5	8	28	22	11	35	8	3
Medicine	4	0	0	0	**	1	0	22	0
Education	11	0	0	0	**	2	0	**	0
Leisure	17	0	0	0	0	0	0	0	0
Origin of culture	**	0	0	0	0	0	10	0	0
National influences	**	0	0	12	0	3	0	0	0
Miscellaneous	11	0	0	3	2	6	20††	16‡‡	0

* Hsiao-tung Fei, *Peasant Life in China: A Field Study of Country Life in the Yangtze Valley* (London: George Routledge and Sons, 1939).
† John F. Embree, *Suye Mura: A Japanese Village* (Chicago: University of Chicago Press, 1939).
‡ George M. Foster, *Empire's Children: The People of Tzintzuntzan*, Smithsonian Institution, Institute of Social Anthropology, Publication No. 6 (1948).
§ Olen Leonard and C. P. Loomis, *Culture of a Contemporary Rural Community: El Cerrito, New Mexico*, U. S. Bureau of Agricultural Economics Rural Life Studies: 1 (November 1941).
** Discussed under other headings.
†† "Town gossip."
‡‡ "Food preparation," 10 percent; "Town gossip," 6 percent.

Ethnographic Studies

In the 1920's, anthropology in this country was still primarily concerned with gleaning remnants of native culture from the American Indians and had little interest in how modern acculturated Indians live. One of the first concessions to the importance of present-day Indians was Mead's study of the "Antler Tribe," [13] a reservation group with a broken-down tribal culture. A few years later, acculturation became an accepted concern of anthropology.[14] The adoption of the contemporary acculturated Indian as a legitimate subject for investigation was induced partly by the disappearance of native cultures, partly by new interests and needs created by the national economic and social upheavals of the 1930's. Much of the first research was carried on under the auspices of the Bureau of Indian Affairs and the Soil Conservation Service, and it was directed toward problems of social adjustment. Subsequently, universities and research institutions sponsored many scientific studies of contemporary Indians, and the resulting monographs may be considered in a broad sense community studies.

The community study approach was first applied to white, Negro, and other groups in the United States more by sociologists than by anthropologists. Studies of American communities were not new, but the era of a consciously cultural or ethnographic approach was definitely opened by the Lynds' studies of Middletown in the late twenties and early thirties. These studies of an industrial town in Indiana covered the culture as completely as any that have been made. Moreover, their problem required historical treatment. The first volume traced changes from 1890 to 1927, emphasizing the effect of technological changes during the twenties, such as the increased importance of the automobile and developments in manufacturing, upon older American patterns. The second volume

---

[13] Margaret Mead, *The Changing Culture of an Indian Tribe* (New York: Columbia University Press, 1932).
[14] Robert Redfield, Ralph Linton, and Melville J. Herskovits, "Memorandum for the Study of Acculturation," *American Anthropologist*, 38: 149–152 (1936).

reported a follow-up study made during the depression, when the Lynds had become quite concerned with the social and economic maladjustments of American life. Although the first survey was a pioneering ethnographic study of an American community, it is a good example of a cultural approach. The Lynds were the first to recognize that one of its principal shortcomings was its failure to relate the town more explicitly and completely to the larger extracommunity society. How to remedy this deficiency in such studies has not yet been resolved: the theoretical and methodological bases for placing any community in its larger setting have yet to be worked out.

Other community studies followed; anthropologists worked with sociologists on some and sociologists worked alone on others. Many of these have such highly specialized interests that they are discussed subsequently under separate headings: Warner's Yankee City series and other studies which are focused on class structure; the Rural Life Studies; and various race relations studies. Some are predominantly ethnographic, but they illustrate a wide variety of interests and methods.

West's *Plainville,* a study of a small farm town in Missouri, is generally ethnographic but, like several other studies in culture and personality made at Columbia University at the same time, it gives much space to the life cycle, or individual development, and very little to economics. Also, it is essentially nonhistorical.

A very different approach is Hicks' study of a small, New England farm town,[15] which he describes with the insights of a journalist and the knowledge of a participant observer, having lived there some years. Intuitive understandings perhaps offset any lacks in explicitness which a social scientist would have provided.

In Latin America most community studies have been made by anthropologists, and following the traditional interest of anthropology, communities were chosen because they preserved

[15] Granville Hicks, *Small Town* (New York: The Macmillan Company, 1946).

considerable aboriginal culture. In the United States survival groups, such as the mountain folk, have interested only folklorists. There is justification for interest in Indian populations of highland Mexico, Central America, and the Andean countries: the race is almost entirely Indian, the language is largely so, and the culture is a mixture of Indian and Spanish. Although the studies concern contemporary peoples they exemplify anthropology's interest in aboriginal cultures, the general objective being to ascertain the interactions of Hispanic and native cultures.

The general problem of Indian acculturation in Latin America, however, is variously conceived and approached. Parsons studied a Mexican community (Mitla) and an Ecuadorian community (Peguche) to ascertain the aboriginal and the Hispanic components of the contemporary culture. Her earlier studies of the Pueblo Indians had demonstrated the presence of many Spanish features in a culture that retained essentially native patterns. Her approach in the Mexican and Ecuadorian studies is largely in the spirit of the older, prefunctional, element-list analysis, and she dissects the contemporary culture into particulars that are respectively of native and of Spanish origin. Parsons' deep intuitive insights save these studies from being extremely mechanical. It is interesting that she makes no use of history or archaeology. Her method is neither functional nor historical; she is not concerned with the processes by which Spanish culture was acquired, nor with the functional relationship of her communities to the larger modern society. Peguche is a kind of dependency of the Spanish town of Otavalo, but information concerning the relationship of the communities to each other is given incidentally rather than through direct analysis.[16]

[16] It is interesting to compare Parsons' account with John Collier, Jr. and Aníbal Buitrón's brief description of Peguche. By means of photographs and only 53 pages of text, the latter give a very vivid picture of the relationship of the Indian community to the white man's world. See John Collier, Jr. and Aníbal Buitrón, *The Awakening Valley* (Chicago: University of Chicago Press, 1949).

PRACTICES 33

The acculturation of Indians under Hispanic influences is approached very differently by Redfield and his colleagues. In the four community studies of Yucatan made under the Carnegie Institution's Maya program,[17] the purpose was to ascertain the effects of a Western European culture upon a folk culture. A kind of polarity between folk and urban communities is conceived in these studies; the four communities range between these extremes and exhibit the functional correlates of the degree of urbanization of a folk culture. A broad interest in how native Indian culture changes under Hispanic influence is present in both Redfield's and Parsons' approaches, but otherwise their orientation has little in common. It should also be noted that the community studies of Yucatan have little connection with the historical and archaeological research that was done under the same Maya program. This shows that a designated unit of research and a single research program do not necessarily lead to integrated results. The terms of collaboration must be clarified in advance.

Several Latin American community studies made by the Institute of Social Anthropology were originally planned as parts of a long-range research program. In 1942, the Institute was developed at the Smithsonian Institution under the writer's direction to carry out basic research on the cultures of foreign areas. The program began with Latin America and constituted part of the State Department's broad plan of Scientific and Cultural Cooperation with the American Republics. It required cooperative teaching and research in Mexico, Peru, Colombia, and Brazil. Dissatisfied with the limited concern of most community studies with special problems, we attempted to place the Institute's research in a larger frame of reference and to develop work that would lead to comparable results.

In Mexico the program endeavored to carry on the Tarascan project, which had been initiated as a cooperative project of the

[17] These four studies are summarized by Robert Redfield in *The Folk Culture of Yucatan.*

University of California and Mexican institutions and planned as an interdisciplinary approach, but had consisted only of the field work of Beals and his co-workers.[18] This project is described below, under *Regional Studies,* though most of the research pertained to communities and the results were published as individual monographs.

In Peru, we envisaged a long-range research program that had specific objectives. If community studies were to be significant and comparable with one another, they had to be planned so that their choice was not based on convenience and personal interest and so that their problems and findings had applicability elsewhere. Two considerations dictated the choice of communities. First, there was the interest in sampling the wide range of cultural types: the predominant national Peruvian culture on the coast, where there are virtually no remnants of folk culture; the strong survival of native Indian or Quechua culture in the highlands; and the aboriginal cultures of the Montaña, the tropical rain forests of the eastern Andean slopes. Second, there was the interest in ascertaining the processes by which the aboriginal or folk societies became assimilated to the Spanish or national Peruvian culture.

The two problems—the sampling of cultural types and the analysis of acculturation—could be combined in a single research program. It was planned so as to begin with central and northern Peru (the native cultures of the southern highlands had been studied previously), and the first step was to make a kind of cultural traverse of northern Peru from the coast to the Montaña. The program began with Gillin's study of Moche, which is the only village on the north coast that is thought of as Indian. Moche is now in the final stage of being assimilated to modern Peru. Later, when Tschopik succeeded

---

[18] Ralph L. Beals, Pedro Carrasco, and Thomas McCorkle, *Houses and House Use of the Sierra Tarascans,* Smithsonian Institution, Institute of Social Anthropology, Publication No. 1 (1944); Ralph L. Beals, *Cherán: A Sierra Tarascan Village, op. cit.*

Gillin as Peruvian representative of the Institute of Social Anthropology, the work was carried into the highlands. Whereas Moche was the only coastal community with any Indian characteristics, the highlands have a great variety of communities, ranging from strongly Indian or Quechua hamlets to fairly modern, commercialized towns.

In order to determine the range of community types and what was most typical of cultural process in the highlands, Tschopik and his Peruvian co-workers, Jorge Muelle and Gabriel Escobar, first surveyed 14 communities.[19] This survey showed that many individuals were being drawn from the small Indian villages to the more commercial Europeanized centers, where they rapidly lost their Indian characteristics to become "mestizos"—a process known locally as "mestizaje." In broader terms this might be called proletarianization. The town of Sicaya best represented this process, and it was therefore chosen for intensive study.[20]

This Peruvian program had in common with Redfield's and Parsons' studies an interest in the changes in Indian culture under Hispanic influence. But whereas Parsons' problem was to segregate Indian and Spanish culture elements and Redfield's was to show how the folk culture of local communities was transformed under urbanizing influences, Tschopik's study was concerned with changes of cultural types, with the effect of nationalizing and proletarianizing processes on individuals who left their home communities and were subjected to national influences. It became a study of commerce, job opportunities, education, military service, social mobility, and other factors which give an individual reared in a folk society a larger horizon and new interests and behavior patterns.

[19] Harry Tschopik, Jr., *Highland Communities of Central Peru: A Regional Survey*, Smithsonian Institution, Institute of Social Anthropology, Publication No. 5 (1947).
[20] This study has not yet been published.

In 1946 it became possible to enlarge the frame of reference of the Peruvian program of the Institute of Social Anthropology by joining forces with the Institute of Andean Research in the latter's plan to make a complete historical, ethnographic, and geographic study of the Viru Valley in northern Peru. Viru Valley is a fertile oasis, which, like other Peruvian coastal valleys, is isolated by complete deserts. The general purpose was to study the valley's cultural development from the time of its earliest inhabitants through aboriginal empires and the Spanish Colonial period to the present day. The clarity of the problem and the division of labor made this one of the most successful cooperative research programs that has been undertaken.

Junius Bird of the American Museum of Natural History worked on evidences of early man in coastal shell heaps and other sites. W. Duncan Strong and Clifford Evans of Columbia University made stratigraphic studies in some of the deeper habitation sites to establish a ceramic sequence by which all sites could be dated. Donald Collier of the Chicago Natural History Museum made excavations in an adjoining area which supplemented the sequences of Bird and Strong. James Forde of Columbia University made ceramic surveys and seriation studies which supplemented the stratigraphic studies on the one hand and dated the many prehistoric sites in the valley on the other. With the prehistoric sites so dated, Gordon R. Willey of the Bureau of American Ethnology studied the development of settlement patterns and of social, religious, and military trends as evidenced by habitations, temples, and forts. Wendell C. Bennett of Yale University studied the development of architecture and cultural features other than ceramics. F. Webster McBryde of the Institute of Social Anthropology studied the geography of the valley, and Allan Holmberg, who had followed Tschopik as ethnologist of the Institute, worked with Muelle and other Peruvians on the contemporary ethnography of the valley.

When the results of this program are published, they will illustrate the value of a cooperative approach to a region. In this case, community studies were fitted into a large program of archaeological, ethnographic, historical, and geographical research. The later phases of Viru Valley's cultural history still need study, and the modern ethnographic studies should be related to Peru as a nation. When these gaps are filled, the project will exemplify at least one ideal of community and area studies. It is true that the basic problems and methods were anthropological, but several specialized anthropological approaches were used, and the project is a convincing illustration of the importance of a central purpose and of the possibility and desirability of teamwork.

The broader dimensions of the Institute of Social Anthropology's program initially called for continuing the cultural traverse of northern and central Peru, so as to complete the general sampling of cultures and cultural processes and also the sampling of southern Peru. Apart from the cultural sampling, the program was originally concerned also with various practical problems which Peru faces: the role of native cultures in modern Peru; the possibilities for readapting the native peoples to new modes of life, as for example by colonizing the new agricultural developments, such as that at Tingo Maria in the eastern tropical forests, with highland peoples; the possibilities of collectivized agriculture or other communal endeavors; the effects of industrialization and mechanization.

In general, all Latin American community studies have been primarily ethnographic and descriptive, and the communities have usually been approached as if they were primitive tribal groups. The published monographs are comparable only within limits, and they are hardly historical at all since no systematic use is made of documentary material to trace culture changes from the Conquest to the present day.[21] They provide excellent source material but they have yet to be related to one another, to historical data, and to archaeology in a broadly comparative approach.

For other parts of the world, community studies are also more ethnographic than historical or comparative. For Japan we have Embree's *Suye Mura*,[22] which emphasizes the social, economic, and religious factors making for family and community solidarity and which is unusual in its attention to the government-controlled schools, farm associations, military organization, and money economy that link the community with the nation. Yang's study of a Chinese village [23] is similarly concerned with the individual community of the present period, emphasis being placed on economics, family organization, and the life cycle. Hsu's Chinese community study is even more concerned with culture and personality than Yang's, virtually the entire book being devoted to family organization and the life cycle. Hsu states that "The present work is an attempt to determine the effects of a Chinese culture on the personality—not the effects of the personality on the culture." [24]

[21] Only three studies have utilized historical data to establish and characterize post-Columbian cultural trends and to analyze acculturation in terms of historical processes: George Kubler, "The Quechua in the Colonial World," in *Handbook of South American Indians*, Vol. 2 (Julian H. Steward, ed.), Bureau of American Ethnology Bulletin 143 (1946), pp. 331–410; Julian H. Steward, "Tribes of the Montaña: An Introduction," *Handbook of South American Indians*, Vol. 3 (1948), pp. 507–533; and Oliver LaFarge, "Maya Ethnology: The Sequence of Cultures," in *The Maya and Their Neighbors* (New York: D. Appleton-Century Company, 1940).

Kubler's article together with Wendell C. Bennett's "The Archaeology of the Central Andes," John H. Rowe's "Inca Culture at the Time of the Spanish Conquest," and Bernard Mishkin's "The Contemporary Quechua," all in the *Handbook* (Vol. 2, pp. 61–147, 183–330, 411–470, respectively), afford a unique analysis of culture change from the earliest prehistoric periods to the present day.

[22] John F. Embree, *Suye Mura: A Japanese Village* (Chicago: University of Chicago Press, 1939).

[23] *Op. cit.* See also Hsiao-tung Fei, *Peasant Life in China* (London: George Routledge and Sons, 1939).

[24] *Op. cit.*, p. 15.

Arensberg and Kimball's Irish study [25] is devoted to the small-farm population rather than to communities as such. The approach is functional, stress being placed on the interrelationship of the family, farm economics, and kinship. Methodologically, its great importance is in the sampling technique used to select the units of field study. From a cultural point of view, however, it is incompletely ethnographic in its omission of material culture, education, religion, political activities, recreation, leisure, and other features.

Social Relations Studies

Class structure. A number of studies, beginning with the Yankee City series,[26] are more concerned with the social status of occupational, racial, and cultural minority groups than with ethnographic analysis. These studies affirm that they approach their subject matter in the manner of a cultural anthropologist, which is true in a sense, but they do not approach it with the same purpose as the cultural anthropologists who have worked on simpler societies. The Yankee City studies are incompletely ethnographic, they are only slightly historical, and they are comparative only to the extent that they laid the pattern for many class studies elsewhere.

The first Yankee City study is concerned with the situational aspects of interpersonal relations. By elaborate statistical procedures all manner of cliques, associations, and other groupings are shown to exist, particularly a three-class system, each class having tripartite divisions. The total cultural behavior of the various groups enters the picture only incidentally.

[25] Conrad M. Arensberg and Solon T. Kimball, *Family and Community in Ireland* (Cambridge: Harvard University Press, 1940).
[26] W. Lloyd Warner and Paul S. Lunt, *op. cit.* and *The Status System of a Modern Community,* Yankee City Series, Vol. II (New Haven: Yale University Press, 1942); W. Lloyd Warner and Leo Srole, *The Social Systems of American Ethnic Groups,* Vol. III (1945); W. Lloyd Warner and J. O. Low, *The Social System of the Modern Factory,* Vol. IV (1947). W. Lloyd Warner, *American Symbol Systems,* Vol. V and *Data Book for the Yankee City Series,* Vol. VI have not yet been published.

The three-class pattern "discovered" in Yankee City is carried over into several other studies, evidently as a stereotype for descriptive purposes rather than as a conclusion arising from the data. It is found in several race studies, despite the necessity of sometimes postulating seemingly missing classes, and it is even applied by Embree to Japan. Curiously, this preoccupation with three classes has not led any of the authors to use a comparative method to postulate theories of culture change that would produce a class system.

Race relations. In most race relations studies the chief interest lies in conflict more than in culture or history, although the monographs differ in the extent to which they are ethnographic and in the amount of emphasis placed on various aspects of their problem. Thus, Powdermaker's and Dollard's studies of the same Negro-white community in Mississippi [27] are similar in seeing interracial relations as a caste situation, with each race subdivided into classes (although they do not agree on class grouping); but they differ in that the former is far more cultural and historical, whereas the latter is concerned with psychological attitudes. In *Deep South* Davis and the Gardners were similarly concerned with the relative status positions and associated attitudes of the two racial groups more than with their culture. It is of interest that one of the Rural Life Studies, that of a southern community of mixed race,[28] has little in common with Dollard's and Powdermaker's works; it is an analysis of community stability rather than of race relations as such and seeks factors pertaining to stability predominantly in farm economics, population movements, and associational ties. Drake and Cayton's study of the Negro in Chicago [29] is also devoted to analysis of the friction points between races rather than to descriptive ethnography.

[27] See footnote 10, p. 27 supra.

[28] Waller Wynne, *Culture of a Contemporary Rural Community: Harmony, Georgia*, U. S. Bureau of Agricultural Economics Rural Life Studies: 6 (January 1943).

[29] *Op. cit.*

The lack of a historical, comparative, and thoroughly cultural approach leaves these monographs somewhat incomplete as basic social science documents. Their findings on race problems are more descriptive than explanatory. If the objective is to destroy prejudice, it would be useful to know the history of race attitudes, which a more comparative and historical approach would provide. Comparisons suggest [30] that race prejudice in the United States has a peculiarly Anglo-American form, which needs to be traced genetically as it became expressed in various cultural and economic situations.[31] If one seeks to break down interracial barriers, it would be useful to know whether cultural differences between Negroes and whites reinforce the separatism demanded by race attitudes. Adequate data are not given in these studies.

Community stability studies. The Rural Life Studies[32] carried out by the Bureau of Agricultural Economics are important as examples of another kind of research in which anthropologists and rural sociologists have participated. They represent a somewhat cultural approach to appraisal of community stability, but they are by no means complete cultural documents. Community stability, which is of great practical importance in farm programs, is judged in terms of economic sufficiency, population movements, such associational groupings as churches, schools, and farm organizations, and various influences from the

[30] See, for example, Donald Pierson, *Negroes in Brazil* (Chicago: University of Chicago Press, 1942).

[31] This approach has been used by Frank Tannenbaum, *Slave and Citizen: The Negro in the Americas* (New York: Alfred A. Knopf, 1947).

[32] The six Rural Life Studies, published under the main title *Culture of a Contemporary Rural Community*, are: Olen Leonard and C. P. Loomis, *El Cerrito, New Mexico*, No. 1 (1941); Earl H. Bell, *Sublette, Kansas*, No. 2 (1942); Kenneth MacLeish and Kimball Young, *Landaff, New Hampshire*, No. 3 (1942); Walter M. Kollmorgen, *The Old Order Amish of Lancaster County, Pennsylvania*, No. 4 (1942); Edward O. Moe and Carl C. Taylor, *Irwin, Iowa*, No. 5 (1942); Waller Wynne, *Harmony, Georgia*, No. 6 (1943). See also the general statement of the purpose of these studies in Carl C. Taylor, "Techniques of Community Study and Analysis as Applied to Modern Civilized Societies," in *The Science of Man in the World Crisis* (Ralph Linton, ed.; New York: Columbia University Press, 1945), pp. 416–441.

"great society." These factors accordingly receive most attention, and there is a corresponding de-emphasis of material culture, the life cycle, religion, and other subjects usually treated in a complete ethnographic monograph.

Perhaps it would not be an exaggeration to say that these monographs illustrate one difference between sociology and anthropology. Certainly, cultural stability cannot be measured by the same criteria as community stability. Communities may become richer or poorer and more or less populous without a profound disturbance of the culture patterns. In fact, although population loss may contribute to community instability—if depopulation is a criterion of instability—it may also bolster cultural conservatism, for it is often the more acculturated persons, those who are assimilated in greater degree to the national culture, who leave the community. This seems to have been the case among the Amish of Pennsylvania, whose cultural deviants, the less conservative, went over to the "great society," while the members of the Old Order clung tenaciously to its past. The Old Order is a case of cultural stability and social instability. The community can be considered stable only if the persons who left it—the rejected, unstable elements—are disregarded.

The distinction between community and cultural stability is brought out in a comparison of Leonard and Loomis' *El Cerrito* and Thompson and Joseph's *The Hopi Way*.[33] The first two authors concluded that El Cerrito was somewhat unstable as compared with the other communities investigated in the Rural Life Studies because of its changing economics, social structure, visiting patterns, and population. Their interest was not primarily to describe culture, and they omitted considerable segments of culture. Thompson, an anthropologist, and Joseph, a psychologist, directed their attention to the stability of Hopi culture and personality. They made no use of a comparative approach and paid only passing attention to economics

[33] Laura Thompson and Alice Joseph, *The Hopi Way* (Chicago: University of Chicago Press, 1945).

and demography, focusing instead on historical, functional, and psychological factors. They showed that Hopi culture had changed little over a long period, that it was integrated functionally by the Hopi view of the world, and that it contributed to an integrated personality type, which they analyzed with the aid of psychological tests. It is of interest that the Hopi, like the Old Order Amish, succeeded in preserving their old culture by rejecting deviant individuals, a process facilitated by the geographical isolation of the Hopi and by the cultural isolation of the Amish.

One may ask whether the concept of community stability, important as it is to agricultural programs, is very meaningful for studies of cultural change. There are scattered conservative communities everywhere, but all communities are experiencing acculturation from world-wide trends. Some communities may disintegrate, for example, Sublette, Kansas; some may disappear entirely, as have many mining towns. Cultural change may be involved, but it is not synonymous with the fate of particular communities. Irwin, Iowa, for instance, is adjudged moderately stable because, while the fairly prosperous farmers have been drawn increasingly into a broader social and economic sphere, sufficient local interests remain to support the community. Irwin has average social stability, but the farm culture appears to have changed considerably, being reintegrated and readapted to that of the nation.

Methodology

Community studies employ a great variety of methods, which are more or less specific to the particular problems being examined, but since this class of studies is essentially ethnographic, four methodological considerations are germane to all of them: (1) the basis of selection of the community; (2) the use of qualitative methods; (3) the use of quantitative methods; (4) the relation of the community to its larger context and the use of data of other disciplines.

Community selection. An implicit assumption of community studies is that the town or village selected is not a unique entity but exhibits something of wide interest. Some of the interests underlying community study have been mentioned: the determination of Indian and Spanish elements in a community culture; processes of assimilation of ethnic groups; processes of urbanization; community stability; race relations; the grass roots of national and political ideologies; and class structure. Whatever the central interest and particular problem, the choice of the community cannot be random—one does not shut his eyes and stick a pin into a map.

Communities are parts of regions and nations. If the formulation of a problem studied in one community is to have significance for other communities or larger groups, the community must be selected on the basis of explicit criteria. The methodological problem here is one of sampling, which has received very little attention in connection with community studies. The choice of the community often tends to be fortuitous; it may be determined by finance, accessibility of the town or village, and other factors which are irrelevant to the problem under investigation.

Three studies, however, have made community selection explicitly a sampling problem. In their Irish study Arensberg and Kimball first used census data to establish class differences in western Ireland, two classes being represented respectively by large and small farmers. They then selected certain communities of small farmers in which to study cultural and social characteristics. The survey technique used in the Institute of Social Anthropology's Peruvian studies, which has already been mentioned, sampled processes of acculturation in the Andean highlands. Another use of the preliminary survey, which was employed in Puerto Rico as described in Chapter IV, sampled regional variation among rural cultures (see pp. 135 ff. infra).

The purpose of sampling need not be merely to select communities which represent cultural types, processes, or other features characteristic of a region. When area and community studies are more fully developed than at present, many of the basic themes of area research which require a community approach will be studied in different parts of the world. Regions and communities will be selected to test hypotheses that are presumed to obtain under specifiable circumstances.

Qualitative methods. An ethnographic method does not necessarily exclude quantification, but it is essentially concerned with qualitative characteristics and in its initial stages has to be qualitative in method. Cultural patterns cannot be described mathematically. The analysis of any community or other sociocultural whole must first be made in terms of structure and function, that is, the features to be measured have to be identified before any quantitative measures can be applied to them.

In the United States, a quantitative or statistical technique is often applied to data obtained by use of a questionnaire. This is possible because of prior knowledge, or assumed prior knowledge, of the principal patterns and features of the culture and society. This procedure cannot be used in cultures that are not known, and attempts to employ it usually illustrate the ethnocentric fallacy of assuming that people of other societies behave essentially like people in the United States.

The field work in community studies must begin with the old and proven ethnographic techniques: participant observation; long, frequent, and directed interviews with informants qualified to give information of special kinds; consultation of archives, records, and documents; recording of case histories; and use of any other sources of information that become available. These field procedures ordinarily require six months to a year or more.

Quantitative methods. The ethnographic or qualitative method must precede the use of quantitative techniques. It is not possible to describe qualitative features and measure them in a single operation. In an unfamiliar society or culture a questionnaire, which is given rapidly by persons who are inadequately trained, who are unfamiliar with the variations in culture, and who do not stay in the community long enough to know and be known by the people, has limited value. There is, however, an important place for the quantitative method in community studies, although it is not a substitute for ethnographic methods, as might be implied from the claims of some who consider a statistical approach essential to science. First, there is need for better sampling of information, and second, for quantification of some features.

It has often been asked with justice whether the number of informants and their selection in certain studies have yielded reliable information. At one extreme, Parsons' account of Peguche, Ecuador, is based mainly on information obtained from a single—and apparently somewhat atypical—villager and on Parsons' own occasional observation of village activities. At the other extreme is Warner's method in Yankee City, where he evidently obtained information on every one of the city's 17,000 inhabitants. Insofar as Parsons was concerned with identifying Indian and Spanish elements in the culture (a non-quantitative problem), her field method has some justification, although the adequacy of her sources of information for her purpose may be questioned. Warner needed adequate samples, for his diagnosis of social classes, cliques, and other groups could not have been made without statistical correlations. Neither Parsons' inadequate sample nor Warner's seemingly excessive sample, however, would have been appropriate for other kinds of problems. If, for example, Parsons had been interested in the importance of subsistence produce as against cash crops in Peguche, in the development of craft manufactures, or in the degree to which national Ecuadorian culture is penetrating the village, she would have needed more sources and different kinds of sources of information, and she would have had to quantify her data to some extent. If Warner had been interested in the functional interrelationship of the total way of life of each social group, the necessary information could have been obtained for a sample far smaller than the total population.

Most community studies lie between these extremes with respect to sampling, and it is no doubt true that their sampling in general is deficient. This may be a carry-over from the anthropological approach to primitive societies, which are so small and so relatively homogeneous that a few informants can actually give a fairly reliable picture of the total society. Modern societies are not so simple. Yet there are often practical reasons for not getting better samples: time is too short and one has to make the most of limited sources; the society may have features which are difficult to investigate for many reasons; an outsider is always at a disadvantage. For example, Powdermaker used 93 informants among Cottonville's 3,000 inhabitants, and all Negro informants were women because local attitudes prevented a white woman from interviewing Negro men. Powdermaker is aware that the study suffered from this fact, but one would doubt that the patterns she describes are seriously biased for lack of better sampling. The methodological deficiency of small samples should not be overemphasized where the problem calls for a qualitative approach.

Adequacy of samples for obtaining such data are difficult to determine in any absolute terms. A native of a village may know every person and be familiar with every aspect of life and yet be unable to give an objective description of the main features of his village. The report of a skilled observer spending a few days in the village is better than no report. A community study that is adequate by all standards will probably never be made. Too many factors are involved to permit blueprinting of a field procedure.

The general lack of quantification of data in community studies also is a heritage of primitive ethnology which was preoccupied with element lists, with analyses of fairly simple groups, and with subjective comparisons more than with measurable differences. But quantitative differences may often amount to qualitative differences, whether one is studying changes within a society or differences between societies. When native populations who have a pattern of subsistence farming come under the influence of industrial societies, they usually begin to produce small quantities of cash commodities to exchange for a few manufactured goods. Eventually, they may depend entirely upon cash crops and imported goods and their entire culture will have been transformed. In each step of the acculturation, however, there are measurable differences which in effect are qualitative differences.

As between societies, differences may spring from the relative importance of institutions and practices which are common to both, and quantitative expression of these characteristics is necessary. A society may have certain essential cultural features, but changes in the relative numbers of people sharing these features may show basic trends. For example, education has long been an American ideal, but the proportion of Americans receiving higher education has increased to the point of representing a profound cultural change. Similarly, the changing proportions of persons who can afford automobiles, who become intelligent participants in local, national, or international politics, and who change their points of view ever so little are quantitative changes that are per se cultural changes. Quantitative changes such as increased length of life may affect culture. The survival of an unprecedented number of persons to an age long past that of useful employment is currently affecting the American family.

To state this somewhat differently, any culture has standards or norms of behavior and it has many deviants. Cultures are changing and they will change in the direction of certain deviants. A quantitative method alone cannot describe the deviants or predict the direction of change, but a series of quantitative studies can supplement qualitative functional studies by increasing the precision of judgments as to the probable directions and rates of change.

Differences between societies may also be partly quantitative. Most American communities have something approximately corresponding to Warner's three social classes, but the proportional representation of these classes may constitute profound cultural differences. Certain suburban communities near New York are predominantly upper class; other neighborhoods and communities are largely middle or lower class; and some are mixed. Middletown had a fair share of all three classes. One of the communities in Puerto Rico, like many American factory or mining towns, has virtually no upper class and a limited middle class. The relative strength of each class in the community in these cases represents cultural differences.

There are other more complex and difficult quantitative problems. A community may be found to be predominantly Catholic. But all Catholics do not belong to the same group in terms of income, school attendance, political beliefs, and many other criteria. An Italian immigrant community may be almost wholly Catholic, and its total way of life may be correlated with Italian background and Catholicism; but in other communities the varied activities and affiliations of Catholics may show quite different constellations of behavior. From a cultural point of view, therefore, the question of the correlates of Catholiscism, Italian background, and many other features which could be taken as basic, constitutes a quantitative problem. If, for example, a qualitative analysis suggests that Italian origin, Catholic religion, and certain other features are associated, there is need to show precisely the degrees of association. The complexity of such relationships has led sociologists to use multifactor questionnaires and statistical procedures.

Relation of the community to its larger context. Community studies have been made almost exclusively by anthropologists and sociologists, the former usually treating the communities as if they were primitive tribes, the latter as locales where certain social problems can best be analyzed. That the community is part of a larger whole which deeply affects it is recognized, but the methodolgy for relating it to the larger whole has not been developed because investigations of regions, nations, and areas generally have divided the subject matter among specialized disciplines. The larger wholes, unlike communities, are studied in terms of their institutional parts rather than as units.

Most field workers are aware of this, but few have made a conscious effort to collect and analyze data which show the relationships between communities and formal national institutions. Of these few, the best examples are Embree's precise specification of the cultural effect of national policies and national economic trends on his Japanese community, Arensberg and Kimball's analysis of the relationship of the Irish small farmer to the larger world, the Lynds' attempt to trace some of the changes in Middletown to national trends, the Rural Life Studies' appraisals of outside influences on community stability, and Ta Chen's efforts [34] to relate Chinese emigrant communities to the national culture. These examine the effects on their communities of national and regional policies; of trends in economic, political, military, and educational institutions, and in industry and commerce; and, occasionally, of social, recreational, and other national developments.

The community is viewed as on the receiving end of these influences. The national sources of the influences and their interrelationship present special problems which involve other social science disciplines. One method of relating community studies to the interdisciplinary approach to the larger whole is suggested in Chapter IV.

[34] Ta Chen, *Emigrant Communities in South China* (New York: Institute of Pacific Relations, 1940).

Conclusions

The community study approach—that of studying all cultural phenomena and their interrelations within the community—has been found useful in connection with many problems. The approach is still defective, however, to the extent that it fails to treat communities within their larger context and to give adequate attention to aspects of culture and society which have national dimensions. That is, the community approach is not yet sufficiently related to that of the various disciplines which study culture in these larger dimensions. It is also strikingly unhistorical in its modern applications. Many problems do not require historical study, but most of those pertaining to culture change and social relations, which are the concern of many community studies, would be illuminated by a historical approach. Finally, community studies are not comparable, for quite unlike purposes underly their problems, methods, and reporting of data.

There is no logic that can or should require research scientists to investigate what does not interest them, and there will undoubtedly be many studies of the community type in the future that are, legitimately, so specialized as to have little bearing on other community studies or on an area approach. At the same time, the community study approach can, apart from and in spite of its various particular interests, constitute an extremely important part of area studies.

If the community is conceptualized as a sociocultural segment of a larger whole, it follows that many of the latter's problems must be studied in the communities. This raises the question of what the major area problems are and how a community study can contribute to knowledge of them. As certain themes of interest develop in area studies, it should be possible to translate them into problems for community study.

The relevance of community studies to area interests in general is that the former may show the local significance of the latter, whether they concern economic trends, effects of industrialization, political ideologies, religious movements, or other aspects. The value of community studies to these larger interests may be illustrated in the case of modern China, where the revolutionary movement is differently interpreted by both scholars and statesmen. The successes of the Red armies and the elimination of the Nationalist Government from the mainland is understood by some persons to mean that China has become Communist in a Russian or orthodox Marxian sense. Present political and military control by a Communist clique can be interpreted as the first step in this direction, but whether this power can be maintained without further fulfillment of promises through complete socialization of economy and establishment of a classless society is an open question. In China, as Owen Lattimore points out, the present Communist regime is supported by the peasants, who constitute 80 percent of the population, and "the primary device in expanding Communist control has been the expropriation of the land of landlords and the richest peasants, and the redistribution of it to poor and 'middle' peasants not as *collectivized property* but as private property." [35] The possibilities of carrying the Communist program further and perhaps even of maintaining it will depend in large measure upon the reactions of the peasant communities.

It is surprising that so little attention has been paid to the peasant communities. For China the only published community studies are those by Yang, Hsu, and Fei. Of these authors, only Fei has been seriously concerned with land tenure and basic economics. Yet any interpretation of contemporary trends in China must ask such questions as: Is the present revolution simply a phase of cycles which have been going on for ages and which are characterized by revolution aimed at redistribution of land? Can rural China possibly collectivize its land

[35] Owen Lattimore, *The Situation in Asia* (Boston: Little, Brown and Company, 1949), p. 158, italics ours.

tenure and land use in view of its family structure, its types of cash-crop production combined with home industries, and its large portion of clan-owned lands? Is collectivization possible without mechanization, supporting, servicing and transportation facilities, and mechanical skills? What does collectivization require in terms of managerial arrangements, marketing outlets, and the like? How would it affect and be affected by Chinese family structure, religion, and local political concepts? Certainly nothing would now shed more light on the meaning of the Chinese revolution than deeper knowledge of peasant communities. Few community studies have been made in China; none have been made of communist towns.

In China, questions concerning political ideology lead directly to questions of community economic adjustments which in turn require analysis of social structure, religion, and all other features of the localized segment of society. Almost any other major theme of current interest can be studied in local as well as in area terms, and most such themes are also applicable to areas other than China. Among these themes are: the effects of industrialization; the possibilities for cooperatives or other kinds of collectivization in relation to mechanization; the economic and social basis of nationalism; the importance of propaganda, organization, and tactics as compared with basic economic and social changes in the development of political and social ideologies; the sources of power which in any government resides in industrialists, workers, landlords, or peasants. Inquiries into these and many other subjects would give greater meaning to a community study in Mexico, Ireland, Peru, China, Brazil or India, for all these areas, despite their distinctive cultural traditions, are experiencing similar trends. All world areas show the effects of industrialization; all are affected by the dissolution of empires and the rearrangement of centers of economic, political, and military power; all show the deep stirrings of nationalism.

REGIONAL STUDIES

It is neither possible nor necessary to review the many definitions of regions.[36] The extent and characteristics of regions, like those of other areas, depend upon the purposes for which they are defined. Regions are generally smaller than major world areas; but for studies of the natural landscape, land use, trade relations, political parties, governmental structures, or of church affiliation, research workers may choose regions of quite different dimensions.[37] There are three principal ways of conceptualizing regions, under which most current concepts probably would fall.

For some purposes a region is conceived as a limited area which has uniformity of natural features: it may be a river valley, plains, a mountain chain, an archipelago, etc. The study of a natural region may include cultural features which are tangible or visible, but such aspects as religion and social organization, which do not form part of the "cultural landscape," are generally given little attention. By the second definition a region is a delimited area which has social and cultural homogeneity; by the third definition it is some kind of structural and functional unit. It is important to distinguish these last two concepts, for while a region may have both cultural uniformity and structural unity, methods of study may differ considerably according to emphasis on one or the other concept.

It has been shown elsewhere (pp. 9-10 supra) that the culture area concept developed from the study of primitive tribes. In limited areas groups of tribes are substantially similar in their

---

[36] Examples may be found by referring to the items in the extensive selected bibliography compiled by Howard W. Odum in "The Promise of Regionalism" (mimeographed), a paper prepared for the University of Wisconsin Symposium on American Regionalism, April 14-16, 1949.

[37] Carle C. Zimmerman, in "Outline of American Regional Sociology" (Cambridge, 1947, mimeographed), makes a tentative effort to block out American cultural regions, but it is based mainly on land use and on cultural values as revealed in novels. It remains to be demonstrated whether regions defined by other criteria would coincide with these.

total way of life, although they may have only minimal relations with or dependence upon one another. The aboriginal tribes of the American Great Plains formed a culture area; the tribes of the Northern Plains formed a cultural subarea or region. If contemporary regions are defined as cultural subareas, the problem is to ascertain the culture or way of life that is found in the different farm groups, communities, towns, factories, mines or whatever kinds of societies make up the region. The part which is chosen for investigation is representative of the other parts.

A cultural approach to a region or cultural subarea would enumerate those common patterns and elements, those uniformities, which distinguish it from other regions within the same general area. The major areas, regions, and smaller units of the modern world, however, are more than territorial divisions in which the cultural content is similar. They are structural-functional units of various kinds, and they are interrelated to one another and to larger area or social wholes. If stress is placed on structural-functional relationships rather than territorial uniformities, any region or other area subdivision may be seen to consist of *unlike* parts, such as town and country or factory and farm, which exist in reciprocal and complementary relationship. A structural-functional approach makes the definition of region infinitely complex, for many kinds of structures and functions have to be taken into account.

In any regional study the cultural content has to be known, but exclusive attention to content is likely to obscure more important relationships. In dealing with primitive culture areas the principal task was to identify and plot the distribution of recurrent patterns and elements. Applied to contemporary society, this procedure is likely to miss the larger patterns. In Latin American studies, for example, Gillin has made a useful preliminary effort to further the study of what he describes as "Creole culture"—an emergent mixture of native Indian and Hispanic cultures, which differs regionally but shows general similarities in such features as Iberian Catholicism, the town plaza, the *paseo,* and ritual kinship.[38] This effort to characterize contemporary Latin American cultures in terms of their native and Hispanic content, like Parsons' endeavors to assign the elements and patterns of her Mexican and Ecuadorian communities to their Hispanic and aboriginal sources, has its value. The study of Latin American culture, both as a total area and as a number of regions or subareas, however, is considerably more than the enumeration of its content. When the native Indian came under Iberian influence, the changes in his life amounted to vastly more than the acquisition of certain Spanish or Portuguese behavior patterns. He became a part of sociocultural systems that were usually larger and structurally very different from his aboriginal sociocultural groups. In some cases, small independent native tribes were absorbed as a labor force in a new kind of economy and society. In other cases, social classes within native empires were readapted to Hispanic empires.

Tschopik, commenting on Gillin's concept of Creole culture, observes that the status in the larger society of what is locally known as Creole or Mestizo depends a great deal upon regional organization or "the framework of a particular local hierarchal structure." In Peru the Mestizo is the aristocrat in class structured Chucuito, where the bulk of the population is predominantly Indian; he is rural in the classless Moche; and he is middle class in the very mixed Arequipa.[39] Tschopik's comments imply that the problem is not only one of defining Mestizo or Creole in terms of culture content but of analyzing the status of the Mestizo in the changing sociocultural whole. Whether the unit of study is a cultural area or subarea, an

[38] John Gillin, "Modern Latin American Culture," *Social Forces,* 25:243–248 (1947); "The Culture Area of Latin America in the Modern World," *America Indigena,* 8(1):31–43 (1948); "Mestizo America," in *Most of the World* (Ralph Linton, ed.; New York: Columbia University Press, 1949), pp. 156–211.

[39] Harry Tschopik, Jr., "On the Concept of Creole Culture in Peru," *Transactions of the New York Academy of Sciences,* 10:252–261 (1947–48).

analysis and description of the whole is necessary. Parsons' people of Peguche, Ecuador, showed a mixture of Spanish and indigenous cultural features. Seen as an isolated community, Peguche could properly be studied in this way. Seen as a part of Ecuador, it is obvious that the villagers of Peguche are potentially lower-class workers and specialized farmers, who have a dependency relationship to the region and to the total structure of the nation.[40] Gillin's Moche is in the last stages of losing its identity as a self-contained village, which preserved Colonial Spanish customs (and a very few native Indian features), and its inhabitants are merging in the social class, occupational, economic, and other groups which, though differing regionally, make up Peru as a whole.

The larger problems require analysis of a great deal more than cultural content. Virtually all modern regions, like modern communities, are linked with a larger structural whole. One of the principal problems of regional studies, therefore, is to examine the nature of this linkage and to analyze the developmental processes that are involved.

It is impossible to review all the studies, in all the disciplines, which pertain to regions, for this would cover most social science literature. Instead, the concepts just discussed will be illustrated with two planned programs of an interdisciplinary nature. The first, the Tarascan project, dealt with the Tarascan Indians as a cultural subarea of Mexico. The second, the Southeastern regional studies by Howard Odum and associates at the University of North Carolina, deals with the Southeastern United States as a cultural and structural part of the nation, emphasis being placed upon problems of interregional interest.

The Tarascan Program

The Tarascan program originated as a joint project of the University of California and Mexico's Escuela Nacional de Antropología and Departamento Autónomo de Asuntos Indí-

[40] This relationship is sketched by John Collier, Jr. and Aníbal Buitrón, *op. cit.*

genas. Ralph Beals of the University of California and Daniel F. Rubín de la Borbolla were the principal planners.

Prior to the inception of this program in 1940, the Tarascan area had been the subject of considerable interest. The area has rich archaeology; its Indians had one of the great empires of native Mexico, the postcontact history saw the replacement of the native empire by Spanish Catholic rule, and Bishop Quiroga was supposed to have attempted to carry out the ideas of Sir Thomas More's *Utopia* among the Indians; and today, the Tarascans form a somewhat distinctive segment of the nation. Former President Cárdenas, who was from the area, was interested in having it studied to show how area knowledge would aid social welfare programs in Mexico. The Tarascan area had been studied from time to time for many years, mostly by Mexican anthropologists and historians, but none of the work had been coordinated with reference to a comprehensive program.

The Tarascan program attempted to plan a basic interdisciplinary study. In 1940–41 Beals and several assistants made anthropological surveys and one community study among the Tarascans. Occasional visits to the area were also made by individuals of other disciplines, but little more was done on the program until 1944, when the Institute of Social Anthropology assigned George Foster, Jr., an anthropologist, and Donald Brand, a cultural geographer, to work on the area in collaboration with their students at the Escuela Nacional de Antropología. Each made a community study. Later, Robert West, who succeeded Brand, made a geographical survey.

Despite the initial hopes and plans, no very significant interdisciplinary studies were made or results obtained. That the results were largely limited to anthropology, the discipline of those who conceived the research and of most of the scientists who worked in the area, was, in the writer's opinion, a consequence of the fact that the particular problems were not conceptualized in such a way that the study provided a definite role for persons other than anthropologists. Partly, too, it was handicapped by lack of funds.

Objectives. The objectives of the Tarascan program were both scientific and practical.[41] The scientific objective was to apply the methods of traditional anthropology to a homogeneous, small, localized, and fairly self-contained people. The focal points were taken as "the ethnology and social anthropology of the Tarasca of today" and the "manifold processes of its rapid modification," with emphasis on economic life. The practical objective was to provide "a body of fundamental data for the administration of the Tarascan area."

The Tarascan area was selected because "until recently [it] was relatively inaccessible and the majority of the [50,000] Tarasca lived in comparative isolation." "A numerous, relatively homogeneous, and compactly situated group is thus available for study under changing conditions [caused especially by the construction of a modern highway], affording an excellent field for social anthropology."

The Tarascan Indians were thus conceptualized as a people with tribal culture, which was beginning to change. The plan called for "the fullest employment of every possible scientific approach." Since the central problem was "to know who the Tarascans were and how they have changed, what their culture was, what their culture is today, and the major steps of the transition from past to present," the methodology included archaeology, use of documents to reconstruct native ethnology and postcontact history, and field study of the ethnology of the modern regional variations (surveys and community studies), linguistics, and physical anthropology.

Nonanthropological disciplines were considered necessary to explain environment in relation to cultural change and admin-

[41] Daniel Rubín de la Borbolla and Ralph L. Beals, "The Tarasca Project: A Cooperative Enterprise of the National Polytechnic Institute, Mexican Bureau-Indian Affairs, and the University of California," *American Anthropologist,* 42:708–712 (1940); Beals, Carrasco, and McCorkle, *op. cit.*

istrative problems connected with land use. It was planned to include geography, botany, zoology, soil studies, agronomy, forestry, grazing, and animal husbandry. Medical and health studies were also considered essential. No provision was made for representation of any of these disciplines in the field parties, for, as Beals intimates,[42] it was hoped that persons making studies in their own disciplines in the area might be persuaded to contribute useful data to the Tarascan program. It was also hoped that economists, sociologists, and political scientists would contribute in the same way. In 1944 cultural geography was added to the field investigation, for it seemed clear that study of many problems of land use lay beyond the ordinary skills of the anthropologist. Budgetary considerations did not permit further additions.

Results. Of the many different studies of the Tarascan area, only a portion are in print. The principal results are four community studies, three of which have been published, and a regional geographic study.[43]

The community studies are essentially ethnographic descriptions of three variant types of local culture. Cherán, in the mountains, is more isolated and more "Indian," that is, more self-contained and culturally conservative. The account is a standard ethnographic treatment of the principal cultural features observable in the community. Tzintzuntzan, a mestizo community of about 1200 persons, is situated on Lake Patzcuaro and is in closer touch with the outside world. With its dependent "Indian" hamlets, it was studied by Foster and several stu-

[42] Wagley, *op. cit.*, p. 11.
[43] Smithsonian Institution, Institute of Social Anthropology, Publication Nos. 2, 6, 7, and 11, respectively: Ralph L. Beals, *Cherán: A Sierra Tarascan Village* (1946); George M. Foster, assisted by Gabriel Ospina, *Empire's Children: The People of Tzintzuntzan* (1948); Robert C. West, *Cultural Geography of the Modern Tarascan Area* (1948); and Donald D. Brand, *Quiroga: A Mexican Municipio* (in press). The bibliographies in these publications cover most of the literature on the Tarascan region. Additional papers on folklore, religion, language, and other special subjects are in preparation.

dents. This monograph is also of the standard ethnographic type, differing from Beals' mainly in greater emphasis on economics (48 percent of its pages as against 36 percent) and in more attention to history; a historical section discusses native ethnography and a concluding section summarizes changes in culture content and organization that have occurred up to the present day. Foster regards Tzintzuntzan not only as a sample of the mestizo Tarascans but of rural Mexico: "The ethnologist thoroughly acquainted with Tzintzuntzan could describe, without ever visiting them, 75 percent of the culture of Mitla or Tepotzlan [the communities studied by Parsons and Redfield]—not only the traits or elements, but their function as well. Or, to put it another way, a typical Tzintzuntzeño could be placed in any one of a thousand other rural Mexican villages, and quietly and unobtrusively he would take his place." [44] Quiroga, another mestizo community, was studied by Brand with the aid of several students.

Foster alludes to some changes in Tzintzuntzan that were caused by the collapse of the native Tarascan empire and he mentions certain ties between the modern people and the Mexican nation. Local factors integrating the area as a whole are hardly touched. The economic reciprocity of communities, which depends upon specialized production in different communities, receives more attention in West's study. West also covers basic geography, demography, settlement types, and methods of agricultural production for the area as a whole.

Appraisal. The following appraisal of the Tarascan program is made in retrospect. None of us could have been wholly aware of the scientific needs ten years ago, and practical considerations would have prevented our meeting many of the needs in any event.

The Tarascan area was conceptualized as a culture area, and consequently the standard ethnographic approach was used,

[44] *Op. cit.*, p. 286.

each community being treated largely as if it were a locally self-contained and integrated whole. If each Tarascan community had been an independent unit throughout its history, the traditional methods of tribal ethnology would have been entirely sufficient. The fact is, however, that the communities have been parts of larger functional units which have changed radically through history.

In pre-Spanish times the entire Tarascan area was integrated by a powerful militaristic empire, of which the many and somewhat differing communities were dependent parts. The Spanish Conquest destroyed the empire, and the missions introduced a wholly new kind of integration. There may even have been some trend toward separatism of communities—some resurgence of folk societies and a strengthening of folk cultures— although there was also some linkage of communities with one another and with the larger Spanish regime in Mexico. This linkage was perhaps more through the social and political power of the church than through military domination or direct political ties. The extent of economic dependency on the nation is uncertain. Spanish influence was so great, however, that Tarascan culture became more Spanish than Indian both in its basic institutions and in its elements. After the strong mission influence there was a period of comparative isolation, but the early Spanish patterns persisted. Recently, but before the era of automobiles and the highway, the area was linked to surrounding areas through trade and to the national government through political controls, land-tenure patterns, and the church. Its people played a prominent role in the Mexican Revolution.

The Tarascan program, like most studies of contemporary communities, did not clarify the nature of the larger, extracommunity, functional whole; it paid little attention to the dependency relationships of the communities and the region to the larger Mexico. The individual communities are fairly tight-knit entities, and all Tarascan Indians evidently have a sense of being one people, a sense of regionalism. Just what the over-all Tarascan structure is today, however, remains to be clarified. The need of the program was first to ascertain whether the region was itself integrated in terms of economic reciprocity, political and church control, common ideology, and other features; and second to use part-time or full-time specialists in economic, educational, religious, and other institutions that have national dimensions. There are still many gaps in specialized knowledge about the Tarascan area; a broad interpretative study has still to be made.

There were certain practical difficulties in carrying out the Tarascan program. After Beals' initial studies in 1940–41, there was no support for the program until the Institute of Social Anthropology sent its personnel to cooperate with the Instituto de Antropología é Historia. The need for study of the Tarascan Indians in their past and present relationships to a larger society had become evident, but the problems required studies beyond the interests or time of the personnel. The program had to emphasize field research, partly because one objective was to train students of the Escuela. The inclusion of culture history and of the studies in other disciplines needed to understand contemporary problems became dependent upon persuading persons to undertake them.

Since some directors of area programs seem hesitant to plan and organize research for fear that scholars will resent "coercion," it is worth mentioning that several students of anthropology at Columbia University have become interested in some of the broader problems of the Tarascan area. A recent study by Pedro Carrasco [45] has analyzed certain aspects of Tarascan religion according to the larger frame of reference suggested here. Instead of regarding the culture of each community simply as a variant of a regional subculture, Carrasco treats

[45] Pedro Carrasco, "Tarascan Religion: An Analysis of Economic, Social, and Religious Interactions," unpublished Ph.D. dissertation, Department of Anthropology, Columbia University, 1949.

Tarascan religion in relation to national Mexican institutions. Historical in approach, this study shows that the interaction of local and national factors produced several different aspects of Tarascan religion. There is traditional folk Catholicism which centers around a system of religious obligations, or "cargos," and saints. This religion stems from early Catholicism, which was introduced when there was communal land to support the cargos. The penetration of the national system of private property, cash crop production, and haciendas led to the loss of both communal and individual lands, which had supported traditional folk Catholicism, and to the growth of two strong national movements, which were in conflict with each other and with the folk religion: (1) the agraristas, who represent government anticlericalism and land reform; (2) the sinarquistas, who represent orthodox national Catholicism.

Carrasco's problem was more than ascertaining Hispanic and indigenous elements in the religion. It was a historical-functional analysis which not only related religion to other cultural factors but also related the community and region to the larger national setting. The thesis is important because it illustrates one way in which studies of both national institutions and of communities and regions have greater meaning if they are brought into relationship to one another.

Were it possible to plan another Tarascan program in the light of our experience, the following projects and problems should be included:

(1) A study of Tarascan prehistory, modeled on the Viru Valley program (see pp. 36–37 supra), that would

    (a) establish a ceramic chronology by means of stratigraphic and seriation studies;

    (b) use ceramics to date other antiquities, such as villages, mounds, irrigation works, and forts;

    (c) interpret these larger remains to show the development of settlement patterns in relation to mounds and temple sites, the expansion of irrigation systems, and other evidences of changes in land use, demography, social structure, and theocratic and militaristic states.[46]

(2) A reconstruction of the native Tarascan culture at the time of the Spanish Conquest.

(3) A series of monographs on the post-Conquest history not only to show culture change in terms of replacement or modification of Indian features by Spanish patterns, but also to analyze the shifting dependency relationships as the community or folk society and culture became integrated with a national Mexican society that had different characteristics at different periods.

(4) A study of the contemporary Tarascan area, modeled somewhat on the conceptual approach of the present Puerto Rico study (see pp. 126–149 infra). The community studies of the Tarascan Indians which have already been made are believed to be adequate samples of the variations within the region. There is now needed:

(a) An analysis of the structure and functions of the region as a whole. This should investigate the extent of local interlinkage through social and religious ties, trade relations, political affiliations and parties, and the like, so as to ascertain whether the area has significant structural cohesion, the respects in which the communities are a functional part of the area, and those in which they are linked directly to the nation.

(b) A study of neighboring haciendas to show any local dependencies between Indians and landlords and any evidence of a class system.

(c) A study of the principal features of national economic, political, educational, religious, and social institutions and ideologies that are affecting the area.

[46] For suggestions concerning some of the problems of such a study, see Julian H. Steward, "Cultural Causality and Law: A Trial Formulation of the Development of Early Civilizations," *American Anthropologist*, 51:1–27 (1949).

(d) A comparative study of Tarascan communities to ascertain variations in cultural features, with special attention to differing local effects of national institutions.

Many of these studies would show the regional significance of national institutions and features. Interdisciplinary cooperation would be necessary, and it could be arranged in a manner similar to that in Puerto Rico.

Southeastern United States Program

Whereas the Tarascan area is distinctive partly because of its heritage from aboriginal times, when it was an independent sociocultural unit, and even more because Colonial Spanish culture has survived there, the Southeastern United States has long been part of a larger whole; and whereas the Tarascan program was developed by anthropologists, the Southeastern United States studies were developed by sociologists, particularly by Howard W. Odum, who has long been identified with studies of regionalism. These facts explain at least some of the differences in the two programs. The Southeastern program is noteworthy because of the conceptualization of the regional unit and the methodology for establishing such a unit, and because it calls for a focus upon a particular problem and for interdisciplinary collaboration.

Concept of region. According to Odum, "The *region*, for purpose of scientific delineation and practical planning, is a major, composite, multiple-purpose, group-of-states societal division of the nation [concept of the larger whole], delineated and characterized by the greatest possible degree of homogeneity [culture area concept], measured by the largest practical number of indices available for the largest practical number of purposes and agencies [quantitative method for establishing a region, see pp. 134–137 infra], and affording the least possible number of contradictions, conflicts, and overlapping." [47] And

[47] Howard W. Odum, *op. cit.*, p. 15.

further, "The larger frame of reference for the conceptualization of regionalism is to be found in the construct of the structural-functional reference of total society or 'the whole,' somewhat after the manner of Talcott Parsons' structural functional theory of relations between the parts and the total in the total system of society." [48]

A region is delineated in terms of culture, structure, geography, political organization, and historical trends. The method for delineating a region is quantitative: "adequate statistical methods applied to a reasonable number of major indices . . . for determining areas of maximum homogeneity . . . The methods proposed for maximizing the homogeneity of states within regions will involve the application at several levels of the factor analysis or principal component techniques for combination of series of single indices into composite indices." [49]

This statistical survey technique has to deal initially with a limited number of features. An interesting difference between this procedure and anthropological procedure is illustrated here. The Puerto Rico project and the Central Andean study used questionnaires to ascertain the limits of cultural regions and to discover the principal dynamic, functional features that were to be studied more intensively by a qualitative method. The initial surveys were made for preliminary orientation. The sociologists who have participated in the Southeastern studies are more interested in quantification as a basic method. In these studies they make a series of statistical surveys, finally achieving complex correlations. The anthropological procedure leads to qualitative studies of communities as samples of regions. The sociological procedure used here leads to an ultimate correlation of correlations.

Odum's criteria of area appear to include features of folk culture and to exclude certain features of national culture.

[48] *Ibid.*, p. 13.
[49] *Ibid.*, p. 14.

That is, regional culture consists of folk culture as it stems from the past and is readapted to national influences. But local manifestations of national technology and political controls—national institutions—represent "sectionalism," not regionalism: "The region . . . is at once an extension and a subdivision of the folk society, characterized by the joint indices of geography and culture and deriving its definitive traits through action and behavior processes rather than through technological functions or areas. The 'South' as a 'section' would comprise the technical, geographic and political 'Confederate States of America.' "[50] As a region, it would include the basic folk culture. The technology of the textile industry puts it in competition with New England, and this situation makes for sectionalism. The social and cultural effects of the textile industries change the lives of the basic population; this change is "regionalism."

Study of particular problems as a regional approach. Odum conceptualizes the Southeast, or any other region, as part of a larger whole which has a certain historical-cultural tradition, geographical adaptations, and uniformities in behavior of the basic population. As such the Southeast lends itself to the study of many problems, and Odum conceives these problems as "of universal interest to all regions and to all students," whether they are race relations, social-industrial relationships, redistribution of wealth and opportunity, standards of living, or class structure.[51] Study of these problems requires the collaboration of a number of disciplines. This is one of the area program objectives, that of "universalizing human knowledge."

As we have suggested previously, study of any social science problem that has cross-cultural implications and does not involve merely the specific and unique relationships and proc-

[50] Howard W. Odum, "Sociological Aspects of Regionalism," a paper prepared for the Round Table on Regionalism, Institute of Public Affairs, University of Virginia, July 10, 1931.
[51] Howard W. Odum, communication to the writer.

esses which, according to the concept of cultural relativity, are found only in a single society requires that the underlying conditions be stipulated. The search for universals or regularities requires a statement of conditions under which they obtain. The research laboratory at the University of North Carolina is quite specific as to the basic characteristics of the subregion to which its hypotheses apply. This subregion includes 13 contiguous counties, "approximating a miniature Piedmont South, with ten counties in North Carolina and three in Virginia." The characteristics of the subregion are as follows: It is predominantly rural, growing cash crops such as tobacco and cotton; because of location it is subject to varied external influences; it is experiencing population pressures; there is a trend toward urbanization (37 percent of the population is urban); half of the farms are tenant operated; industry is infiltrating, especially textile mills and tobacco factories; it has a comparatively low wage rate for workers and a low standard of living; it has a low level of education and a high rate of illiteracy. The subregion of the Piedmont, which has these characteristics, is a "laboratory" for interdisciplinary study of many problems which have cross-cultural significance.[52]

Like the research programs for most areas or subareas, the list of major problems for study is really a list of themes of interest. The specific terms of integration of the different disciplines with respect to these themes have yet to be specified. The themes and related research projects are discussed under the *Problem Approach,* pp. 83–94 infra.

Conclusions

"Region" has many meanings, each of which reflects a special interest and many of which are based on a single factor—economic, geographic, political, or other. For interdisciplinary

[52] University of North Carolina, "Preliminary Descriptive Prospectus: Subregional Laboratory for Social Research and Planning" (mimeographed, January 1, 1940).

area research, however, region has to have the fullest possible multifactor definition, based on all aspects of behavior and hence including all disciplines; else regional research would be unidisciplinary or merely multidisciplinary. A cultural definition which makes a region simply a cultural subarea in the sense that it has uniformities, or consists of similar parts, is inadequate since another definition of the same region may emphasize its structural unity and the heterogeneity and functional reciprocity of its parts. Few regions, however, are independent units, and it is necessary to take into account the dependency of the region upon the larger sociocultural system.

The methodology of regional studies must be adapted to the different kinds of institutions and the different types of integration found within a region. In the Tarascan region a great deal of culture is integrated on a community level and it can best be investigated by the community study method. In the Southeastern United States the penetration of industrialization is introducing many special features which cut across communities, and study of these features requires region-wide surveys. Both these regions, however, may be regarded as cultural subareas, which have certain uniformities or common denominators of behavior that can be ascertained by comparisons of communities or by studies of social classes, occupational groups, or other "horizontal" divisions of the regional society. Thus, the Tarascan region is distinguished by certain features derived from both the aboriginal and the Colonial Spanish heritages, and the Southeastern United States by a type of Anglo-American folk culture.

An understanding of the structural unity of the region as a whole and its dependence upon the larger society requires an interdisciplinary study of the institutions which function on both a community and a national level. The Tarascan region of aboriginal times was an independent society made up of specialized, reciprocating parts—artisans of different kinds, military, theocratic, and social classes, and a centralized

PRACTICES

administrative organization. Today, the region has lost much of its structure and internal specialization. The community functions more in a national than regional context. Cash crops are produced for and manufactured goods are bought in a national market; local specialization and exchange have diminished. The people are members of a national church and governmental system, of which the region is only an administrative unit. The farmers are peasants in a national structure of social classes. The Southeastern United States never had complete structural independence or unity. Like the post-Conquest Tarascan region, it was economically and politically dependent upon a larger society, but it differed because its greater size and internal complexity entailed heterogeneous and reciprocating parts, such as town and country. More recently, the penetration of industrial institutions has introduced such contrasts as factory and farm. Tarascan society must be viewed as a comparatively homogeneous, loosely structured group of folk communities within an agrarian state, whereas the Southeast is a more heterogeneous structure of specialized groups, whose folk culture is being nationalized by the institutions of an industrial state.

National Studies

Area research which deals with modern nations differs from that which deals with primitive tribes, communities, regions, and cultural areas in that the subject matter, however heterogeneous and complex, usually has a relatively high degree of unity which follows from state sovereignty.[53] A nation has

[53] There has never been and there is not likely to be agreement on the definition of "nation." A primitive nomadic band, a preliterate horticultural community, a Luxembourg, an Indonesian sultanate, a China, a United Kingdom, a Russia, or a United States are all nations by one definition or another. From the present theoretical point of view, they have in common mainly the fact that each is clearly delimitable in its own terms as a unit or whole in which political, social, ideological, and other phenomena can be studied and integrated to some extent.

definite boundaries, a central government backed by some power structure, and a set of laws which produce certain regularities in the functions of national institutions. This is true even of satellite nations, which are economic or political dependencies of more powerful states. In the field of international relations one has to be concerned primarily with the "capabilities and intentions of sovereign states," which usually but not always act as units, maneuvering according to their concepts of self-interest and drawing upon their total economic, military, and political potentials. A nation is also a natural unit of investigation because census data, statistics, historical documents and compilations, and many other kinds of information are usually available on a national basis.

It does not follow that because a nation is a relatively clearcut entity, and because vast information is available on a national scale, the terms of interdisciplinary cooperation are thereby prescribed. Modern nations are heterogeneous and complex, and are being studied by a great variety of specialists. How shall this diversity of information be integrated?

In practice the integration of national studies, in the writer's opinion, has been dictated by international relations, by the necessity of formulating United States foreign policy. Among the pressing questions have been: What are Russia's intentions, tactics, and military strength? How can the spread of communism in Southeast Asia be halted? How can the sympathetic allegiance of India to the cause of democratic nations be insured? These questions can be broken down into many more specific inquiries, and each can be answered in part on the basis of available knowledge. A theory of integration of the social sciences may not be involved. Nonetheless, theoretical problems are implied, for these questions are among the basic themes of interest which potentially orient interdisciplinary procedures.

The considerable success of governmental wartime agencies

in dealing with practical questions demonstrated the value of coordinated research. Social science theory as such was not directly involved, but a thorough analysis of the work of the Office of Strategic Services, the Office of War Information, and special branches of the State, War, and Navy Departments probably would reveal a great deal of implied theory. Such an analysis would be a considerable task, for few of the results have been published and some of them may not yet be declassified. It is quite clear, however, that the principal problems these agencies had to solve can be grouped among the basic themes of interest which orient interdisciplinary area research (these are discussed on pp. 86–94 infra).

There are hundreds of interpretative and integrative books about nations, and practically all of them are the products of individuals. Works covering a wide range of knowledge were common in the era of universal scholarship. Today, specialization has gone so far and accumulated knowledge is so great that general interpretation has become an extremely difficult task for an individual. From Herodotus to Marco Polo and on through world explorers, such as Alexander von Humboldt, individuals with a breadth of information, first-hand experience, or perhaps mere enthusiasm wrote general accounts of peoples, nations, and areas. More recently, scholarship has become so specialized that interpretative works tend to bear a disciplinary stamp. Even such general accounts of the United States as those by Lord Bryce, John Gunther, John Dos Passos, or Frederick Lewis Allen are specialized in approach, presentation, and point of view.

One recent volume which is at least partly the result of an area program is John K. Fairbank's work on China.[54] In viewing this book in relation to Harvard University's area program on China, several facts must be taken into account. First, Fair

[54] John K. Fairbank, *The United States and China* (Cambridge: Harvard University Press, 1948).

bank is a student of China and he has a vast background of knowledge. Second, the book is one of a series on foreign areas, "The American Foreign Policy Library" edited by Sumner Welles.[55]

The focal point of Fairbank's interpretation of China lies in the general theme of international relations—that is, China's bearing on the position of the United States in the contemporary and future world. Interest in this political objective is shown by the auspices of publication, by Sumner Welles' "Introduction," by the opening chapter entitled "Our China Problem," and by the concluding chapter entitled "American Policy Toward China," in which the problem is seen partly as one of countering the spread of Communism and in which recommendations are made for furthering the principles of "individual freedom" and "individual political liberty." The contents of the book are clearly selected and oriented toward political action. Of 340 pages, 210 deal with recent China in terms of its relationship to the Western world and of internal processes of change. Early phases of Chinese development, which are the central concern of historians and Sinologists, are included to show the background of the contemporary scene but they are accorded minor space. Geography, economics, community studies, and social structure as such are not major subjects of interest. Data in these fields, however, are included as they bear upon the central theme, which is the meaning of China's nationalism and of China's position in the international world.

Fairbank acknowledges his indebtedness to the participants in the Harvard China program, "which has tried to mobilize in one series of discussions both the expert's knowledge of China and the methods of the social scientist." Whatever these

[55] Among the volumes in this series published by the Harvard University Press are: Dexter Perkins, *The United States and the Caribbean* (1947), and Arthur P. Whitaker, *The United States and South America* (1948).

participants contributed, the interpretation is undoubtedly Fairbank's; and it must be supposed that the organization and emphasis as well as the conclusions are affected in some degree by the fact that the author is an American writing to illuminate United States foreign policy.

Several questions may be asked of any national area research program: To what extent is foreign policy the predominating concern? If it is the predominating concern, how far can area research be dedicated to this purpose without endangering the objectivity of social science itself? If area programs have other purposes, which are purely scientific rather than political, what are they? Is there one theme or are there many basic themes of scientific interest? Can all these themes be encompassed in a single interpretative work, or does each call for separate treatment?

*National Studies and
the Social Sciences*

The scientific challenge of area research is to weave together the threads of knowledge from many special fields of scholarship. Since social science has become highly specialized, any national study is almost inevitably made from a particular viewpoint, even though the research worker commands vast knowledge. Even the more general interpretative works tend to bear a disciplinary stamp, or else to reveal a political or social point of view.

The distribution by subjects of a considerable number of books about nations is suggested by the following tabulation of the individual items in the bibliographies in recently published short sketches of Japan, China, and India and Pakistan: [56]

---

[56] Douglas G. Haring, "Japan and the Japanese, 1868–1945"; Francis L. K. Hsu, "China"; Daniel and Alice Thorner, "India and Pakistan"; in *Most of the World* (Ralph Linton, ed.), pp. 814–875, 731–813, 548–653, respectively.

	Japan	China	India and Pakistan
History	5	3	2
Economics	3	7	6
Government	2	3	2
Geography	2	1	1
Language	0	0	0
Literature and art	7	0	2
Novels	0	0	6
Religion and philosophy	5	0	5
International relations	0	1	2
Law	0	0	0
Sociology	0	3	3
Anthropology			
Community studies	2	5	4
Culture and personality	3	0	0
Ethnic groups	0	0	4
Education	1	0	0
Demography	0	1	2
Militarism	2	0	0
General interpretations	5	6	6
Bibliographies	1	0	1

The bibliographies tabulated, of course, represent partly the authors' own interests—Haring and Hsu are anthropologists and Thorner a historian and wartime analyst of India for the Foreign Broadcast Intelligence Service of the Federal Communications Commission—and partly the differences between the three countries. With respect to area programs the interesting fact is that of the disciplines represented in most of them, only history, economics, government, geography, literature and art, and religion and philosophy have such clearly defined fields that books come under these headings. The bibliographies list few works on the sociology or anthropology of nations; instead, there are studies of ethnic groups, social structure, communities, and culture and personality. For reasons mentioned later a book on the anthropology, i.e., culture, of a nation is either ambitious or else very specialized. It is of further interest that demography, education, and militarism do not enter area programs as special fields of study, though they are covered in most general books on nations.

Finally, of all the bibliographic references given for these nations, only about 15 percent are of a general nature, cutting across many disciplines; and most of these are political or propagandistic. It would be difficult to name one that is not slanted toward a discipline or toward a social point of view. There are many studies of nations which represent vast learning—for example, the Beards' studies of the United States, Latourette's, Creel's, Laufer's, Wittfogel's, and Bishop's on China, or Sansom's on Japan,[57] but all these persons are essentially cultural historians. One might mention also two recent works on Latin American nations—Smith's on Brazil and Whetten's on Mexico [58]—which, in any general classification, would be placed under "rural sociology," for both deal essentially with the rural populations.

The role of anthropology in studies of nations requires some comment because anthropology is not specialized like other disciplines. Whereas a study of national economic, political, or social institutions would present clear and delimitable problems, a study of national culture would include everything; and while anthropologists do the entire task for primitive tribes, it is a formidable undertaking for contemporary nations.

[57] Charles A. and Mary R. Beard, *A Basic History of the United States* (New York: New Home Library, 1944); Kenneth S. Latourette, *The Chinese, Their History and Culture* (New York: The Macmillan Company, 1946); H. G. Creel, *The Birth of China* (London: Jonathan Cape, 1936); Berthold Laufer, *Sino-Iranica* (Chicago: Field Museum of Natural History, 1919); Karl A. Wittfogel, "The Foundation and Stages of Chinese Economic History," *Zeitschrift für Sozialforschung*, 4:26–60 (1935); C. W. Bishop, *Origin of the Far Eastern Civilizations*, Smithsonian Institution War Background Studies No. 1 (1942); G. B. Sansom, *Japan: A Short Cultural History* (London: The Cresset Press, 1931).

[58] T. Lynn Smith, *Brazil: People and Institutions* (Baton Rouge: Louisiana State University Press, 1946); Nathan L. Whetten, *Rural Mexico* (Chicago: University of Chicago Press, 1948).

Anthropology's solution is to approach nations in two rather specialized ways. First, it treats the nation as a culture area—as a unit which has a common denominator of similar beliefs, customs, and behavior patterns, rather than as a structural-functional whole which consists of heterogeneous and reciprocating parts and institutions. Second, some anthropologists emphasize "national character," an approach which stems from the recent interest in culture and personality.

When a nation is approached as a culture area, there is little place for consideration of the interacting national institutions and sociocultural segments, whose analysis would require virtual omniscience on the part of any research worker. Distinguishing culture traits and patterns claim attention, and the emphasis varies somewhat with the individual scholar.

Three books on nations, all modest in scope, were produced by anthropologists as a result of World War II. Lowie's book on Germany [59] is a general cultural description written by a person of broad scholarship and considerable knowledge of Germany. Mead's sketch of the United States [60] was written with war morale in mind, and it deals principally with the assimilation of ethnic minorities to the national pattern and ideology. Embree's systematic description of Japan [61] was also written to give general information, as were the short sketches of nations and areas contained in the Smithsonian War Background Studies.

Most of the World [62] is a collection of summaries of nations by several anthropologists. In general, they tend to approach the nations from the culture area point of view, that is, they emphasize those features and patterns which constitute a common denominator of culture and may be observed throughout

---

[59] Robert H. Lowie, *The German People: A Social Portrait to 1914* (New York: Farrar & Rinehart, 1945).
[60] Margaret Mead, *And Keep Your Powder Dry* (New York: William Morrow and Company, 1942).
[61] John F. Embree, *The Japanese Nation* (New York: Farrar & Rinehart, 1945).
[62] See footnotes 38 and 56, pp. 56 and 75.

the nation, for example, material culture, family structure, foods, etiquette, religious beliefs, and the like. They pay comparatively little attention to formal political, economic, military, educational, and other national institutions.

Wagley's article on Brazil covers its history, racial and ethnic composition, the differences between Brazil's six regions, and the common denominator which constitutes the national culture. "Japan and the Japanese, 1868–1945," by Haring, similarly emphasizes features that give homogeneity to the nation: geography, race, population, food supply and preparation, house types, clothing, settlement pattern and social relations within the settlement, etiquette, interpersonal relations, family, social classes, religion, literature, art, education, government, and economics. The last seven subjects have national as well as local aspects.

In "China," Hsu pays somewhat more attention to national institutions. He includes not only resources and population but land use, land tenure, handicrafts, industrialism, distribution of wealth, family, social classes, government bureaucracy, religion, and education. Compared with Fairbank's account,[63] Hsu's is less historical, less interested in China's relations to outside peoples—the alien rule of conquering peoples, the Western political and economic impact, and modern political relations—and less concerned with the internal processes of revolution and nationalism. Hsu's section on acculturation touches some of these subjects among a greater variety—law, education, family types, recreation and sport, living conditions, communism, and, in another section, missionization—and he sees them as posing a problem of reconciling the conflicting behavior and values of East and West.

A cultural approach to contemporary nations which would be comparable with that to primitive tribes would presuppose virtual omniscience; anthropologists have to advocate that which they cannot do. How to interrelate the data of all dis-

[63] *Op. cit.*

ciplines in national terms is still baffling. Meanwhile, a fairly recent trend in anthropology has given the somewhat spurious impression that it has found the key to national studies in analysis of "national character." A considerable number of people seem to have the impression that anthropologists regard such analysis as the principal purpose of area research or as anthropology's main contribution to such research. Studies of so-called national character have great value, but it is important to understand their relation to other approaches.

Interest in national character is but part of a broader interest in culture and personality, which underlies many studies of primitive and other peoples throughout the world. Linton, Kardiner, Du Bois, Mead, Hallowell, Benedict, Haring, Kluckhohn, Bateson, and Gorer, among others, have written extensively on the subject.[64] The purpose of the studies is to ascertain how culture affects personality, that is, how the different kinds of personalities encountered in different parts of the world result from distinctive culture patterns. It deals with the "individual"—the typical individual—because, while the particular modes of behavior are culturally determined, they are actually integrated by psychological processes which can only be studied in individuals. The theoretical importance of this approach is discussed in Chapter III, under *Integrating Concepts*. The practical value of understanding national character is of course very great. Any American dealing with foreign

[64] Among the earlier studies of this type were Abram Kardiner, *The Individual and His Society*, and *The Psychological Frontiers of Society* (New York: Columbia University Press, 1939, 1945); and Ralph Linton, *The Cultural Background of Personality* (New York: D. Appleton-Century Company, 1945). The field has expanded so rapidly that two recent works reprint collections of essays: Clyde Kluckhohn and Henry A. Murray, *Personality in Nature, Society, and Culture* (New York: Alfred A. Knopf, 1948), and Douglas G. Haring, *Personal Character and Cultural Milieu* (Syracuse: Syracuse University Press, 1949). Otto Klineberg, in *Tensions Affecting International Understanding*, Social Science Research Council Bulletin 62 (1950), has made an excellent critical appraisal of the methods of studying national character, or "character in relation to nationality."

peoples will find that they react in quite unfamiliar and unexpected ways. He needs to understand their attitudes and motivations—the psychocultural mainsprings of their behavior.

Studies of national character have to take into account the general culture patterns of the particular nation, but are not primarily concerned with structure or function. Some of the more extreme applications, for example Gorer's studies of the United States [65] and of other modern nations, make child training the principal determinant of adult or national personality and therefore of national behavior. They attribute little importance to historical, economic, political, social, and other causes. Interpretations of why Japan or Germany went to war which are based on toilet training or weaning have been criticized for their failure to take nonpsychological factors into account.

Studies of national character are at present pioneering explorations of a new field and are still uncertain in two respects. First, their psychological assumptions are controversial. Different schools of psychology make different assumptions about what factors determine personality structure and about the extent to which personality can be modified after childhood. Second, the cultural factors selected as determinants of personality are greatly oversimplified. National culture is represented as if it were homogeneous, as if the same factors affected personality in all regional, ethnic, racial, occupational, class, professional, and other segments of society. Possibly in the case of old and slowly changing societies, like Japan, China, or India, there are still basic common denominators of culture and personality which are found throughout the society. The writer would guess, however, that differences within many societies are more important than similarities. For example, in Puerto Rico the upper class may be fundamentally more like upper-class continentals than like the laboring class on a

[65] Geoffrey Gorer, *The American People* (New York: W. W. Norton & Company, 1948).

corporate-owned sugar plantation, while the latter may have more in common with Hawaiian pineapple workers than with San Juan's elite.

A rather well-known work which represents the simplified view of national character is Benedict's book on Japan.[66] Benedict sees Japanese society as a hierarchy of relative statuses, each member reacting in a conventional way to persons above him and below him. The individual always exhibits one set of attitudes and behavior patterns when confronted by a person in a superordinate position, and another toward a person in a subordinate position. His attitudes and behavior patterns respecting authority are learned in childhood. Benedict wrote her book on the basis of wartime information gathered while she served the Office of Strategic Services. Her problem had been to understand what there was about Japanese national character that gave Japan a united front during the war and how this understanding could be used in the peace settlement. For such practical purposes, the common denominator of Japanese behavior was the primary consideration.

That all Japanese were enough alike to be a formidable foe in war does not mean that the characters of Japanese of all kinds actually conform to a national stereotype. There are undoubtedly differences between town and country, between owners and workers (whether on farms or in factories), and between persons with ideologies which survive from the old feudal systems and with those which derive from a capitalist system. Embree's study of a Japanese community showed that modern commercialism was beginning to disarrange the older system based on social rather than financial status.

Much finer discriminations of subtypes of national character and of differential cultural factors creating these subtypes are needed to keep this approach abreast of area studies.

The National Research Council's Committee on Asian Anthropology, recognizing some of the scientific needs in the

[66] Ruth Benedict, *The Chrysanthemum and the Sword* (Boston: Houghton Mifflin Company, 1946).

field of "Personality Structure (Norms)" as well as its practical value, states:

> A basic factor in estimating the direction of social change in an area is the personality structure dominant in it. With the exception of a little preliminary work on the Japanese, Chinese, Siamese, and Burmese personality structures (which needs expansion and refinement), this field is encumbered with stereotyped judgments that obscure rather than illuminate the important area of psycho-cultural relationships. Once launched, such studies are susceptible to infinite refinements based on class, regional and ethnic groupings. Any projects along these lines, however limited, may be useful if only for comparative purposes. It is probable that such studies might be most profitably pursued as a part of studies in national integration . . . or as studies suggested in community organization . . .[67]

National character studies may be important in an area approach, for they attempt to show how psychological factors integrate and give drive to culturally-determined ideologies and values, whether political, theological, philosophical or social. It is not their general problem at present, however, to explain the origin, structure, or function of national sociocultural patterns, and they consequently cannot be considered anthropology's only contribution to area research. The cultural approach to a nation requires that varied national phenomena be interrelated. These phenomena pertain to many disciplines, and there are many different terms of integration. National character studies represent only one, which, as ordinarily phrased, calls for the cooperation of anthropology and psychology but is necessarily concerned with the contributions of other disciplines.

The "Problem" Approach

Two points of view about the role of research problems and interdisciplinary cooperation have been mentioned (pp. 17–19):

[67] National Research Council, "Research Projects Recommended by the Committee on Asian Anthropology," Final Revision (mimeographed, May 24, 1949), p. 4.

Some persons believe that imaginative planning can and should formulate new kinds of problems which call for genuine teamwork in research. Others conceive an area program to be one in which several disciplines participate, each carrying on its traditional kind of research; they consider it sufficient that participants work on the same area and under the same auspices.

In practice, neither extreme is actually followed. On the one hand, no problem has yet been conceived so broadly that it gives just weight to all disciplines and unity to all area data. There is no single area problem, but many area problems. For example, the development of nationalism may be phrased as a problem for research requiring data from many fields; but nationalism is only one of many area interests. On the other hand, narrow disciplinary problems, numerous and varied as they are, are not chosen whimsically and at random. The predominance of certain current interests has led individual research workers in different fields to choose their problems with reference to common goals, even though they may not make this fact explicit and their research may not be directly related to that of fellow scientists. These general interests or objectives, in preceding pages, have been called "basic themes."

The contemporary world has become an integrated whole, that is, one area or "one world" to the extent that events in each region, nation, or area affect and are affected by events in many other places. A study of Pan-Islamism cannot be separated from British colonialism or from nationalism in India, and developments in India deeply affect England's external economic and political developments. If one studied Chinese peasants instead of Pan-Islamism with its socioreligious focus, the subject would also have international ramifications: the meaning of Chinese communism and nationalism to the peasant population; the locus of political power; how communism and nationalism are related to internal factors of demography, food supply, social structure, governmental forms, and processes of revolution; and to external factors of foreign trade, infiltration of political ideologies, military power, and international policies.

These interrelated features of a complex and rapidly changing modern world have inspired innumerable interpretative works by many kinds of persons. In social science they have created certain general interests which underlie the greater part of research, whatever the scientist's field of specialization. They are not specific problems; they are not logical or mutually exclusive categories of area phenomena or disciplinary specializations; and they do not have equal importance from scientific or practical points of view. They are simply foci of interest, which the social scientist, like anyone else, has to consider in investigating current affairs. Any listing of these themes is quite arbitrary because they merely represent points of emphasis in a continuum of interacting phenomena and overlapping interests. Other points of emphasis would be equally logical and justifiable.

From the point of view of interdisciplinary area research, the important fact about these themes of interest is that each calls for a great breadth of knowledge. Each involves the others; none is a self-contained disciplinary problem. Some of the current themes are: international relations; nationalism; economic development (rural and industrial); colonialism; demography; urbanization; power structure; the effects of industrialization on backward people; social structure; relationships between ethnic and racial groups; and the development of philosophical, ideological, and value systems.

All these themes have practical aspects, for they underlie decisions that have to be made concerning public policies. But, in view of the rather widely held belief that social science can rescue humanity from its badly snarled relations, it is important to clarify what science can and cannot do. The improvement of health is a humanitarian objective, and science can clarify the medical, dietary, economic, and social factors that affect health. There still remain such practical questions as who pays for medical services and, insofar as health is related to diet, who eats less in order that others may eat more if there is not enough for all. If the world is quite unlikely to be able to provide enough for all in view of present and probable future population trends, science can do little more than point out some of the implications of world trends. A program dedicated to raising the general standard of living would confront the problem of redistribution of wealth. On such questions the final action depends upon social values, and science cannot prescribe it. Similarly in the field of international relations science can explain world trends, predict the intentions and capacities of nations and peoples, and state the probable results of action taken, but it cannot, as science, say what decisions should be made.

The following list of themes is not exhaustive. It includes some of the principal interests that are current in area programs, in order to show how each is related to the others and how each may underlie research problems on which careful planning is needed for effective interdisciplinary collaboration.

International relations: In a very broad sense this theme encompasses all others, for while international relations may be viewed in restricted terms of world trade, diplomacy, the spread of ideologies, or war, they are also affected by and affect the internal development of each nation and area. For example, the relations of the United States and Russia to each other and to East Asia, a key world area, cannot be understood without knowledge of what is happening inside China. Such studies as those by Fairbank and Lattimore [68] as well as books and articles by journalists, observers, novelists, and writers like Edgar Snow, Agnes Smedley, and many others make this fact amply clear.

Knowledge of events inside China or any other nation or world area requires a wide variety of research. Whether the

---

[68] John K. Fairbank, *op. cit.;* Owen Lattimore, *The Situation in Asia.*

ultimate motivation of such research is to guide policies of the United States or of the United Nations or whether it is to further scholarship as such is probably an academic distinction. The important fact is that scholars and laymen now want to know about the same kinds of things.

The theme of international relations in the narrower sense of the external relations between nations is a topic which enlists the research of various disciplines. (See pages 3–4 supra for the contributions of "international relations," "political institutions," and "literature" at Columbia University to knowledge of relations between the United States and Soviet Russia, and the relevance of other studies made under the headings of economics and history.)

Nationalism: Interest in the development of nationalism appears in almost every area research program, and it is probably safe to surmise that this is so because trends toward nationalism are a striking characteristic of practically every contemporary world area. Lattimore's use of nationalism as an interdisciplinary research problem has already been cited (page 19).

So far as nationalistic political parties and ideologies are concerned, study of the problem would fall mainly within the traditional domain of political science. But a purely institutional and ideological approach would miss many basic factors which cut across the fields of other social science disciplines. The growth of nationalism is affected by types of farm production, industrialization, local resources and economic potentials, internal and external trade relations, ownership of property and distribution of wealth, levels of living (especially as compared with aspirations about standards of living), colonialism, import-export quotas, and any number of other economic factors. It is also affected by changes in national structure, which are in turn induced by economic and other factors; by realignments of occupational and social classes; by changes in regional relationships; and by value systems.

The National Research Council's Committee on Asian Anthropology states,

> This problem [of the influence of the central government on rural life] is basic to an understanding of new forces in Far Eastern social life. It is closely allied with new developments in national self-consciousness. In a country like China the differences of this impact in Kuomintang and Communist areas . . . would be of particular interest. The success or failure of many new programs for national unification, economic planning or the depth of nationalism as a social force in Asiatic countries will depend largely on the nature of the impact of the central government on the masses of the population.[69]

National structure: A shift of emphasis readily changes the interest from nationalism to national structure, although many of the same facts are involved. National structure can be studied in a rather formal analytic way, the purpose being to identify the various sociocultural groups and institutions which constitute a nation. Knowledge of the functional dynamics of the parts of a national structure requires studies of communities, regions, social classes, economic institutions, governmental systems, foci of power, national philosophies, and the like.

The precise task of each discipline, however, depends upon the nature of the whole; the Pueblo Indians, Paraguay, and the United States would have to be approached differently. In a heterogeneous and changing modern society, the political ideologies may vary and the locus of political power may shift among the various social, occupational, ethnic or other component groups. Nationalism or any other effective ideology depends upon sufficient grass-roots support, and such support can only be understood in terms of the multiple economic, social, and cultural factors that affect each part of society.

The National Research Council's Committee on Asian Anthropology comments under the heading "Changing Aspects of National Structure":

[69] National Research Council, *op. cit.,* p. 4.

The chief goal of such studies would be to gauge the importance and direction of social changes associated with the appearance of new social groups. More specifically, projects would involve studies of the rise of new class systems, including social, industrial, labor, youth and ethnic groups in relation to traditional group adjustments and to the bearing of these new groupings on political and economic problems of the area. . . . studies on the effects of increasing urbanization as well as the absorption of minorities are of major importance. For example, industrialism is a question which may be approached from the background of many fields but whatever the point of departure it is important to understand the traditional versus the new role of labor as well as the new role of management and capital investment in both their traditional and changing aspects. Similarly, the growth of new bureaucratic, military, capitalist, and intellectual groups are of equal importance in some areas of the Far East. Also, the rationale of the new Indian political amalgamations and their impact on the total structure of Indian life are of immediate significance. Obviously any project would have to limit itself to a particular area of amalgamation. The role of intrusive groups like the European, Chinese, and Indian minorities would also fall into the scope of this general type of problem.

In this range of problems the persistence of colonial impositions should not be neglected. For example, the Spanish class structure in the Philippines persists to the present and deeply affects the base line from which national structure will develop.

The urgency of this problem is greatest where the growth of new and influential groupings has developed farthest and yet has been largely neglected, namely India, China, and Japan. However, to understand the full range of current re-adaptations of Asiatic cultures such problems should be undertaken in all stages of their development, from the nascent aspects in countries like Burma and Siam to the more fully developed aspects found in Japan, India, and China.[70]

Value or ideological systems: Another shift of emphasis from nationalism would focus interest on what are variously called value, ideological, or philosophical systems. Values, goals, or aspirations are greatly affected by economic and social circumstances, and therefore may vary among the different socio-

[70] *Ibid.*, pp. 3–4.

economic components of a nation. They are affected by traditional religious or philosophical systems, so that within any nation a great religion like Catholicism or Confucianism may have tremendous power in shaping trends. Peoples of different nations may find a strong bond in such movements as Pan-Islamism. Values are also expressed in political movements like communism or democracy, and in socioracial movements like Pan-Africanism. The interaction and balance of all these factors constitute national and area values or ideologies. Studies in the humanities, especially philosophy, religion, literature and language, as well as the data of history, political science, and virtually all the social sciences bear on problems of values.

To quote again from the Committee on Asian Anthropology:

> Since consciously held and unconsciously operative values are among the most active social forces, any project which suggests comparative analyses of religion, philosophy or ethics may be of importance. Only through an understanding of such beliefs, explicit and implicit, may it be possible to formulate bases for understanding the integrative forces within any one community and arriving at bases for universal accord. The assistance which historians, humanists and philosophers can render psychologists and anthropologists in such studies calls for collaboration between such specialists to explore properly such problems.[71]

At the Harvard University Russian Research Center, for example, a special project on the Communist Party is directed by Merle Fainsod.[72] As the Communist Party represents the dominant national ideology of contemporary Russia, the subdivisions of the project are of interest in showing some of the specialized approaches to this central theme. The project includes studies of the composition and structure, both formal and informal, of the Party. It deals with focus of power, leadership, ideology, relationship to Russians who are not members

[71] *Ibid.*, p. 4.
[72] Russian Research Center, Harvard University, "Programs and Census of Current Projects" (mimeographed, January 1949).

of the Party, to law, the military organization, education, means of propaganda, literature and the arts, history, nationalism, economics, science, trade unions, peasants, and consumers. Communism is also being studied as a world movement in projects covering its meaning in Europe, China, and elsewhere.

Economic change: Most of the modern world is experiencing continuous and rather fundamental economic change. Whether economic factors are considered basic to other kinds of change or not, their importance in relation to most contemporary world trends is such that they merit detailed attention. The subject of economic change is too broad to be more than a general interest, and for research it has to be broken down into many specific topics. Some of the principal subdivisions are rural economics, industrial development, and foreign trade. Each may underlie innumerable specialized economic studies but each also involves other disciplinary interests.

In area research the subtheme of rural economics is exemplified in studies of production and consumption but, in a broader sense, it includes land use (cash and subsistence crops, fertilization, mechanization, and other methods of production, marketing, and credit); land tenure; farm community organization (competition, cooperation, collectivization, etc.); levels of living; farm population; rural-urban and rural-national relationships; rural cultural types, values, and ideologies. None of these rural features can be understood without reference to national and international factors.

National studies in economics include not only the foregoing but such topics as national income, industrialization, banking, credit and public finance, internal trade, foreign trade, natural resources, and concentration of economic power. National economics may be a focus of interest, but it could easily shift in one direction to national political power, law, social structure, and philosophy, which sanction it, and in another direction to international trade, finance, and political and military relations.

Demographic trends: Many parts of the world have had sharp population increases in the last century and especially in the last few decades. There are probably several causes of these increases, among them improved public health and sanitation, new farm crops and better farming methods, and industrialization and urbanization. There are also important consequences or potential consequences: population pressures, lower levels of living, internal and external migration, readiness to accept radical political, economic, and social ideologies, expansionist foreign policies to relieve internal pressures, changes in local communities and in social structure, and others.

The importance of "population shifts" in Asia has been stated by the Committee on Asian Anthropology as follows:

> Changes in the size and/or location of population groups may be the key to other culture changes suggested in this paper. They will need to be studied in all their aspects among which the economic will be highly important. Questions of health may prove significant and should not be forgotten. Projects along these lines can be envisaged as ranging from some with wide socio-political implications like the displacement of the Hindu and Moslem population in the Punjab or the tribal disturbances in Kashmir to less explosive ones like the drift of Annamese populations westward and southward in the Indo-Chinese peninsula. Philippine experiments in resettlement in Mindanao or similar Dutch experiments in Indonesia are worth extensive study in the effectiveness of conscious and planned reform. A definitive and highly instructive study of the influence of the Chinese population shift to the west and back again as the result of the recent war in the Far East deserves attention. The Japanese deportation of labor groups during the war, like that of the Javanese into Malaya, must have repercussions of considerable importance.[73]

Urbanization: The trend toward urbanization is a worldwide phenomenon, and the processes and consequences of urbanization and its relations to industrialization, trade, and other developments have become subjects of general interest. Urbanization may be approached from many points of view.

[73] National Research Council, *op. cit.,* p. 3.

Redfield, for example, in his study of Yucatan [74] was concerned with the effects of urbanization upon folk culture. How industrial societies in general affect rural populations is a broader interest, or subtheme. Howard Odum states the urban-rural problem in terms of the development of new occupational groupings as a result of urbanization. A related approach would be concerned with the cultural contrasts between rural and urban groups. Another point of emphasis in the same general interest is the focus of power.

Urban-rural contrasts clearly involve many interrelated problems which could orient field work of many kinds. For example, in the community studies previously described rural communities were seen as local sociocultural segments which are losing political power (the Tarascan communities of Mexico, Peguche in Ecuador, and Moche in Peru), as communities which are losing their local distinctiveness (Sicaya in Peru), as communities whose members are becoming secularized, individualized, and disorganized (Redfield's range from folk to urban in Yucatan), or as communities which have an economic reciprocity with urban centers.

On the other hand, urbanization may be seen not only as a contrast to rural life but as a process governed by its own laws of zoning, differentiation, competition, and the like, as in the urban ecological studies of Park, Burgess, McKenzie, and others.[75]

As a theme, urbanization is somewhat more diffuse than the others which have been discussed and its wide meaning allows many special approaches. These are closely related if urbanization is conceptualized in an interdisciplinary sense, for all the rural-urban contrasts and all the processes of urbanization result from economic, social, political, and other factors that affect entire nations.

[74] Robert Redfield, *The Folk Culture of Yucatan*.
[75] R. E. Park, E. W. Burgess, and R. D. McKenzie, *The City* (Chicago: University of Chicago Press, 1925); R. D. McKenzie, *The Metropolitan Community* (New York: McGraw-Hill Book Company, 1933).

Race and ethnic relations: In a logical sense, perhaps, race and ethnic relations fall under the general heading of national structure. Their practical importance in the contemporary world, however, has made them the subject of special emphasis in many area studies. The general theme of racial and ethnic relations breaks down into certain subthemes in research programs. Many sociological or psychological studies examine the points of tension between racial or other minority groups. Others emphasize the cultural and psychological factors which support normative attitudes and which give vitality and resistance to different cultures. Some students are more interested in the processes of assimilation of minority groups, such as the national minorities in the United States, the ethnic and racial groups of Russia, or the Indians of Peru or Mexico. The problem may be how these people are acculturated to national patterns of behavior, how they fit into the national structure, or both. It is part of the much broader problem of change in both the parts and the whole of any society.

Regional contrasts: Cultural and social contrasts between regions were one of the subjects studied by Odum's group working on the Southeastern United States. Robert Wauchope has indicated that a similar general problem serves as the frame of reference for the various disciplinary studies made under the auspices of the Middle American Research Institute at Tulane University. One of the problems in Middle America is to study the contrasts between coastal plain, piedmont, and mountains in racial population, social organization, economy, political history, religious background, and other respects.

The nine general themes described above represent foci of interest. A different emphasis would require somewhat different phrasing of purpose. There are any number of themes in addition to those mentioned, and when some of these are sufficiently developed, they too will become major interests.

CHAPTER III

SOME CONCEPTS AND METHODS
OF AREA RESEARCH

Some of the problems and practices of area research have been surveyed in preceding chapters. The present chapter will attempt to present a unified theory and method of area research. This should be considered a tentative rather than an ultimate formulation; it is hoped that it will be provocative.

INTEGRATING CONCEPTS

Any area program, whether of training or of research, requires the participation of many disciplines. It is certainly true in research and presumably true in training that the data of the different social sciences and of the humanities have to be integrated if an area program is to consist of more than a miscellany of unrelated facts. The present uncertainty about integrating concepts may mean that social science is still in a "natural history" or phenomenological stage.[1] Preoccupation with "facts" or with description in area research is evidence of scientific immaturity.

"Integration" has no fixed definition;[2] its meaning depends upon the problem in hand. For present purposes, we shall take integration to mean a functional interdependence of social science and humanistic phenomena within some kind of organizational whole or system. At the first national conference on the study of world areas sponsored by the Social Science Research Council, Pendleton Herring and Talcott Parsons implied that an area whole is something like a biological organ-

[1] F. S. C. Northrop, *The Logic of the Sciences and the Humanities* (New York: The Macmillan Company, 1947).

[2] Pitirim A. Sorokin, *Society, Culture, and Personality* (New York: Harper & Brothers, 1947), pp. 337–341, reviews some of the meanings of integration (and disapproves of them all).

ism: it was their suggestion that "study of an area, its culture, and its society" might entail cooperation of many disciplines somewhat like that in medical research.[3] This does not mean that area research need adopt the biological analogy, for there are important differences between biological organisms and social systems. Both, however, are organizational wholes, although areas or territorial units are not necessarily self-contained entities like biological organisms. A community, a region, a nation, or any other area society may be a whole only in a relative sense; its organization, though incomplete, may be sufficiently definite to make it the frame of reference within which a variety of phenomena interact. The questions for area studies are: What kind of interaction is meant? What kinds of integrating concepts are appropriate to area wholes? What kinds of problems require such concepts?

The writer's concept of integration is only one of many that underlie various area research projects and it is necessary to examine some of the others. The natural area is not an integrative concept, for it sets no criteria for inclusion or exclusion of phenomena. Among the more important and current integrative concepts are the individual, culture, and society. More specialized concepts, such as value system, philosophy, and ideology, are emphasized in particular studies, but these are parts of culture—they are master patterns of society, rather than something separable from both society and culture. The individual, culture, and society are here selected as the principal integrating concepts requiring comment because, where social science method is concerned, area studies tend to focus upon one of these. The three concepts are of very different orders.

The Individual

Failure to distinguish two different concepts of the individual has caused some methodological confusion in social science.

[3] Wagley, *Area Research and Training, op. cit.,* p. 5.

The concept of the individual as the "carrier of culture" and the concept of the "cultural personality" have been used as if they were identical. Because culture has no real existence apart from the behavior of actual people, it is sometimes argued that the personality structure of the typical individual is an indispensable feature of any study of society or culture. "Personality," "society," and "culture" may be brought into relationship for many purposes, but they are very different kinds of constructs and the respective integrating processes vary greatly.

In any social science study the individual's behavior and products are the basic observable phenomena from which constructs of particular societies and cultures are derived. These constructs are norms or abstractions rather than directly observable phenomena, but they are based on observations of the varieties of behavior exhibited by different individuals. Study of social and cultural behavior deals with individuals as the components of society and as the carriers of culture but not necessarily as psychological entities. The structural and functional whole is social, and the integrating processes are sociocultural, not psychological.

Research problems in which the individual is conceived as the integrative whole are of a different order. The purpose of the previously mentioned studies of cultural personality and of national character was to ascertain how socially inherited modes of behavior are integrated within the typical individual. Whether the society and culture are primitive, with fairly stereotyped behavior patterns, or are contemporary civilizations, with considerable variation in possible behavior and therefore need for choice, the various economic, social, and religious modes of behavior are synthesized, reconciled, or patterned within each person. Every individual acquires a personality structure and tends to find a way of life that involves a maximum of direction and integration and a minimum of internal conflict. The concrete terms of personality structure depend upon the culture, but the processes of personality integration are psychological. They presumably are equally applicable to all people. The different personalities result from psychological adaptation to the sociocultural and natural environments.

If the problem is simply how culture and society affect personality, the inquiry is essentially psychological and does not have direct bearing on broader social and cultural interests of area studies. This problem could also be stated, however, as the effect of personality structure on cultural change. Approached from this point of view, the problem would be to ascertain how established personality types eliminate, select, and recondition new modes of behavior. It would be assumed that a society cannot accept new modes of behavior which are too inconsistent with or cannot be integrated into the prevailing personality types. The problem of how personality affects culture, however, cannot be stated as if culture and personality constituted a closed circle. If, as some studies seem to claim, personality and adult behavior result essentially from childhood training which in turn is determined by culture, it would appear that culture merely creates personality and personality merely perpetuates culture. Obviously there are factors in change which have to be analyzed in social and cultural terms, and while personality undoubtedly conditions change, it cannot be assigned the dual role of cause and effect.

Culture and Society

Culture is generally understood to mean learned modes of behavior which are socially transmitted from one generation to another within particular societies and which may be diffused from one society to another. A society is a particular group of people whose relationships have a special pattern, but there is no such thing as society in the abstract, for the nature of any such group is determined by its cultural heritage. Culture on the other hand does not exist without societies, and societies have no forms or functions that are not determined by culture. Society and culture are different though complementary concepts. There has been a confusion of culture areas and social wholes, and of cultural change and social change.

In dealing with primitive cultures the anthropological unit of study is a "tribe," which is a society—a structural-functional whole. But many cultural problems have extrasocietal dimensions. Much of the cultural-historical approach has dealt atomistically with culture elements, such as firemaking, metallurgy, agriculture, the family, religious practices, or art styles. Each of these elements may be studied in isolation, being traced through time and space. That a great many elements have about the same territorial distribution gave rise to the concept of the culture area. A culture area, however, is not a society; it includes a number of societies which share a similar way of life. Culture area consequently is not an integrating concept but a descriptive device which presents the common denominator of behavior of several societies.

Studies of primitive cultures led to the concept of culture pattern [4] or configuration, which requires the corollary concept of function,[5] for patterns are means of describing the functional interrelationship of all cultural phenomena or the master plan of a society, even though the criteria of patterns vary. Culture areas as wholes are not integrated by patterns, although they are often approached as if this were the case. Any world area is characterized by a culture and a pattern, but the area is not necessarily an integrated whole and the pattern is not the integrative factor of the culture area. A culture area is a territorial division within which a particular pattern, like any specific culture element or complex, recurs in each

[4] Ruth Benedict, *Patterns of Culture* (Boston: Houghton Mifflin Company, 1934).

[5] "Function" has been conceptualized in many different ways by Radcliffe-Brown, Malinowski, and others. In its simplest meaning, function merely signifies that cultural phenomena are interdependent and interact within some kind of social unit.

of the different societies. Because no two societies are exactly alike, the pattern of a culture area represents merely an abstraction or common denominator of the patterns of the societies within the area.

The various nations of the West, such as Germany, England, France, Greece, or the United States, have different individual patterns, each representing the particular way in which economics, social institutions, political attitudes, and ideological systems are organized and integrated. Distinguishing the West from the East involves a high degree of abstraction. Western science, logic, industrialization, capitalism, political democracy, and many other features are functionally interdependent in the pattern of Western civilization. This does not mean that the West is an integrated whole and the East another whole. It means merely that Western societies have a number of general features in common which distinguish them from Eastern societies. These general features and patterns are abstractions of the more particular and diversified ones which occur in each independent society or nation.

Culture pattern, therefore, is an integrating concept only when applied to particular societies such as nations. It is not the integrating concept for a culture area unless the societies within the area have such interdependence that they form a larger whole, a supersociety coincident with the area. The nationalistic trends in Southeast Asia would be no more than recurrent political and ideological patterns within a culture area—an area of "political pressures"—unless an organized state emerged. The Indonesian Republic represents a step toward formal area unity. Nationalism in India has meant separatism, but the societies and nations of South Asia have, as W. Norman Brown points out (cf. pp. 10–11 supra), important economic, political, cultural, and religious ties. These may someday cause the culture area to develop into an organized whole, in which all parts fit a single pattern. China was split into two states during its revolution. The functional interdependence of world areas has become so great that in 1943 a United States presidential candidate could write about "one world," a term that has since been used increasingly often. The intersocietal or international connections that give some functional unity to culture areas and the interarea connections that are leading toward one world have not yet become clearly patterned. In fact, they are so fraught with confusion that the literature on area trends and world trends shows considerable disagreement about what is happening.

The differences between the concepts of society and culture mean that social change and cultural change, though closely connected, must also be distinguished. Societies may experience rather drastic changes of certain kinds without any important alteration of their culture. These are sometimes called "social interaction" as contrasted with "social" or "cultural change." Baseball furnishes a rather simple illustration of the difference between social and cultural change. As a cultural institution baseball has certain fairly fixed characteristics: competitive teams, rules, loyalties, and, in the professional leagues, commercial aspects and pageantry. Each team may be considered a society. Within the rules of the game the teams may win or lose; their ailing athletes, the strategy of their managers, and many other factors make for success or failure. Their changing positions within the league represent rather considerable social change. But the fate of a particular team need not in the least affect the rules. The culture of baseball is in fact such that some teams must necessarily succeed at the expense of others in order to perpetuate the pattern. If a certain team is a consistent winner, the proportions of a ball park may be altered to make competition fairer; or if attendance declines, a livelier ball may be introduced or new rules made. But any changes in the culture of baseball are relatively minor and they are devised to perpetuate its basic pattern of fairly equal competition. In any case, what happens to the teams—the societies— does not greatly affect the rules, or culture. But any change in the rules may greatly affect the teams; and in baseball or any organized sport a change in rules is accepted only after extended discussion by participants, whose welfare may be threatened.

The difference between social and cultural change, illustrated in the case of baseball, is equally applicable to other subgroups of a society. In Euro-American societies, for example, there is a pattern of "free enterprise" and competition between business institutions, and whether these are corner grocery stores or international oil companies, the competition is supposed to be based on generally accepted rules. In the nature of things the success of one institution must be at the expense of others. The culture which prescribes the terms of competition is of course not static; but it is significant that when cultural trends begin to favor certain competitors, for example, when monopolies begin to develop too rapidly so that an undue number of competitors succumb, the total society makes an effort to strengthen the pattern of free competition—that is, to halt cultural change —by adjusting the rules so that all competitors have a more equal chance.

The distinction between social and cultural change is important in historical studies, for cultural history is by no means the same as national history. To illustrate the point again by the theme of competition, a culture area may be characterized by patterns of competition between the nations within the area, as in Western Europe. The successes or failures of individual nations which result from the strength or weakness of their rulers, the intrigues of ministers, the strategy of generals in certain battles, and various political maneuvers may be no more than expectable episodes within the cultural framework. All nations cannot win any more than all baseball teams can lead a league. The fate of the individual nations, like the fate of baseball teams, is rarely the same thing as the fate of civilization, a change in culture. A historical approach which interprets the rise and fall of nations or empires as the growth and decline of civilization fails to make this essential distinction.

The rise and decline of the kingdoms in the ancient centers of civilization in Egypt, Mesopotamia, India, China, Meso-America, and the Andes is often described as the development and fall of civilization. It is true that the particular kinds of societies found in these centers did not survive, but most of the basic cultural achievements, the essential features of civilization, were passed on to other nations. In each of these centers both culture and society changed rather considerably during the early periods, and everywhere the developmental processes were about the same.[6] At first there were small communities of incipient farmers. Later the communities cooperated in the construction of irrigation works and the populations became larger and more settled. Villages amalgamated into states under theocratic rulers. Meanwhile building arts, ceramics, metallurgy, weaving, urban planning, writing, astronomy, mathematics, and other fundamentals of civilization were developed. Finally, culture ceased to develop, and the states of each area entered into competition with one another. In the Near East, Mesopotamia and Egypt were culturally stagnant from the Bronze Age (about 3000 B.C.) until the Iron Age, some 2,000 years later. China changed surprisingly little from about 1000 B.C. until one hundred years ago. In Meso-America and the Andes, culture was comparatively frozen between 1000 A.D. and the Spanish Conquest.

When culture ceased to change greatly in these centers, an era of cyclical conquests followed. The conquests conformed to a fairly stable cultural pattern, which was not unlike that of the competition of baseball teams within a league. Each state began to compete with others for tribute and other advantages. One or another state succeeded in dominating the others, that is, in building an empire, but such empires ran their course and collapsed after some scores or hundreds of years only to be

[6] Julian H. Steward, "Cultural Causality and Law: A Trial Formulation of the Development of Early Civilizations," *American Anthropologist*, 51:1-27 (1949).

succeeded by another empire not very different from the first. The peak of each empire brought a kind of richness and splendor; between empires, there were "dark ages" and local independence.

For the historian this era of cyclical conquests is filled with great men, wars and battle strategy, shifting power centers, and other social events. For the culture historian the changes are much less significant than those of the previous eras when the basic civilizations developed, or, in the Near East, those of the subsequent Iron Age when the cultural patterns changed again and the centers of civilization shifted to new areas.

The concept of culture is being used in historical studies, but the distinction between social and cultural change is not always clear. Toynbee, for example, writes about the growth and decline of "civilizations," but whether he is dealing with societies or cultures is often quite obscure.[7] It is not surprising that he finds something mysterious and even metaphysical in the decline of early "civilizations" because, failing to distinguish the fate of societies from that of culture, he often seems to mean the decline of nations, not of culture. In a similar way, Spengler reflected the pessimism of Europe after the first world war in writing about the "Decline of the West" as if culture itself had declined rather than particular states, which had lost out in world relations according to the prevailing competitive culture pattern.

A sharper distinction between society and culture would be of assistance in more precise formulation of some of the basic problems of modern world trends. Much of the competition for economic or political power has occurred within the framework, or rules, of a general culture. The industrial revolution brought profound cultural change to Western Europe and caused competition for colonies and for areas of exploitation. Japan entered the competition as soon as she acquired the gen-

[7] Toynbee, Arnold J., *A Study of History*, Abridgement by D. C. Somervell (New York: Oxford University Press, 1947).

eral pattern. The realignments of power caused by Germany's losses in the first world war and by Italy's and Japan's in the second are of a social order. What new cultural patterns will result from these changes remains to be seen.

The general assumption today seems to be that we are in danger of basic cultural change caused by the spread of communism. Russia acquired drastically new cultural patterns as a result of her revolution. Whether communism has the same meaning in other nations has still to be determined. The Chinese revolution, for example, could be regarded from two extreme points of view: first, that it is essentially an agrarian revolution, a phase in the cycles of Chinese history which have been repeated again and again within a fairly stable cultural framework that has persisted since the Ch'in or T'ang dynasty; second, that it is a completely new ideology, an entirely new cultural pattern, imported from Russia. Certainly neither explanation is the whole truth, and the outstanding contribution of Fairbank's study is its examination of the processes of revolution and Chinese nationalism to ascertain to what extent the trends conform to China's traditional past and to what extent new patterns are being introduced.

Studies of smaller societies or segments of societies may also fail to distinguish society and culture. In our review of community studies (pp. 39–43) we have seen how many monographs were concerned with social relations within established patterns rather than with cultural patterns themselves. The contrast between social stability and cultural stability, as illustrated by the Old Order Amish of Pennsylvania (p. 42), shows the need to distinguish social and cultural change.

The distinction between society and culture does not mean that both concepts are not necessary to area research. Culture determines the characteristics of societies and it can only be observed as it is manifest in particular societies. Cultural change almost inevitably causes social change, although the reverse may not always be true.

The distinction between society and culture has several methodological implications. First, culture can be used as an integrating concept in area research only in the case of particular societies. Culture areas which consist of many societies are integrated wholes only in a loose sense. Second, the concept of society requires the corollary though distinct concept of culture, for social change does not necessarily involve cultural change. Third, the nature of any social change is determined by the basic culture and can be dealt with effectively only in terms of culture. Whether the objective is to stop the ravages of competition, eliminate the evils of business cycles, or correct any other social ills, the solution must deal with the basic pattern and not merely with the limited phenomena which are determined by it.

Sociocultural Wholes as Integrative Levels

The various kinds of societies whose structure and function are determined by the cultural heritage of the world areas in which they exist are *sociocultural* systems or wholes.[8] A sociocultural system is a unit, the social segments and institutions of which have a significant degree of interrelationship and functional interdependence. Any given sociocultural system, however, is an empirically derived construct which represents a particular kind of society in a particular developmental continuum, that is, within a designated world area. Research problems and methods, therefore, have to be adapted to sociocultural systems which are characterized (rather than classified) with reference to two criteria: (1) the cultural tradition which they carry; (2) the relationship of the parts to the whole within the level of development. The first criterion depends upon the

[8] *Sociocultural* has various other shades of meaning. For example, Sorokin *(op. cit.)* makes society, culture, and personality an "inseparable trinity." For reasons previously stated, the writer considers personality an integrative concept of a different kind than the concept of a sociocultural whole, even though personality is produced by and may affect a sociocultural whole.

principle of cultural relativity. The second requires a theory of sociocultural levels within a developmental continuum.

Within any world area there is a developmental continuum of sociocultural wholes or systems. More complex and territorially larger systems supersede simple localized systems. In the progression from simple to complex, the earlier units and the earlier cultural practices do not entirely disappear. There are survivals of what Sumner and others call "folkways" and "mores" and "folk societies" and "folk cultures." There has been a strong tendency to treat these survivals as if they were preserved like fossils and functioned in the newer sociocultural wholes more or less as they did in the older. For example, the concepts of community and folk society are treated as though they represented absolute and universal entities, whose study requires identical methodology regardless of whether they are independent sociocultural units or dependent parts of larger wholes, which latter vary according to the cultural tradition of the areas in which they are found.

This tendency to apply a given methodology to any "survival" is a result of the assumption that the higher levels of sociocultural systems differ from lower ones essentially in complexity. Because systems of the higher level do not consist merely of more numerous and more diversified parts, it is methodologically incorrect to treat each part as though it were an independent whole itself. For example, in the early eras of Peruvian culture, communities were independent sociocultural wholes but later these communities became dependent parts of states or empires. Still later they were incorporated into the Spanish state of Peru. Today Peru is strongly aboriginal Indian in many respects and also preserves many practices of sixteenth century Spain. But modern Peruvian culture is not simply a mechanical mixture of elements and patterns of aboriginal Indian, old Spanish, and contemporary Euro-American culture; and Peruvian society cannot be regarded as a structure made up of strictly native villages, of purely sixteenth century

Spanish communities, of modern cities, and of various economic, religious, and political institutions. The older cultural elements, communities, and institutions have undergone qualitative changes, brought about by their functional dependence upon a new kind of whole. A continuum of development is recognizable in Peru's history, but it consists of successive levels—the lines may be drawn at various points—that are parts of a whole which is qualitatively new as well as quantitatively more complex.

In science generally, there is good precedent for dealing with levels of integration. The distinction between the inorganic, organic, and superorganic is a very old concept and it means that the sciences dealing with each level frame their problems in terms of special aspects of phenomena. Thus, biology involves principles and processes in addition to and different from those found in chemistry and physics, for the organization of matter known as life has qualities peculiar to itself. Psychological phenomena, although based on neurological structures and functions, have some aspects which are best investigated in terms of themselves, that is, at a psychological rather than neurological or organic level. The particular forms of human behavior known as culture involve something more than psychological processes, and consequently culture patterns and complexes may properly be studied in terms of themselves, that is, through distributional, historical, and comparative methods which represent operations on the superorganic level. Because behavior patterns are concretely manifest in particular groups of people or societies, whose structure and function they determine, sociocultural units represent levels of organization which are not wholly reducible to biological, psychological, or even cultural phenomena.

If the basic concept of levels is valid—and this would not seem to be very debatable—types of sociocultural organization no less than the phenomena of the inorganic and organic levels must be divided into sublevels. In physics, for instance, it is much more convenient to study the behavior of gases as wholes than in terms of each molecule or atom. Even a field equation, which will someday interrelate all physical phenomena in a single formula, will be a poor tool for dealing with everyday problems of mechanics.

In biology the concept of sublevels is extremely important. Sublevels differ according to the nature of the whole, and in each sublevel the principles of organization and the relationships between the parts and the whole are different.[9] The lowest form of unicellular life has properties that are not reducible to chemistry and physics, for life has the distinctive quality of self-perpetuation, which is not found in inorganic matter. Even if a living cell could be created synthetically, it would nonetheless be more practicable for many purposes to treat its life processes in terms of themselves. Multicellular organisms consist not merely of cells, but of specialized kinds of cells, each of which has distinctive functions and relationships to other kinds because they are all dependent parts of new kinds of wholes, of higher levels of organization. The cell is incompletely understood if it is not studied as part of an organ; and an organ is intelligible only as part of a total organism. The heart, for example, has specialized cells, which function according to principles of chemistry and cell metabolism; but the heart serves to pump blood in the body, while being affected by respiration, nerve impulses of various origins, hormone content of the blood, and other factors.

This concept of levels is not an argument against reductionism, for there are many problems in all the major divisions of science where reduction of one kind of process to another is not only valid but desirable. Where levels of organization mark divisions between sciences, such reduction often represents an important interdisciplinary approach. Thus nutrition, originating in biology, has utilized chemistry to the point where

[9] Alex B. Novikoff, "Integrative Levels in Biology," *ETC.: A Review of General Semantics*, 2:203–213 (1944–45).

many foods, vitamins, and other essentials can be produced synthetically. Similarly it could be argued that ultimate explanations of cultural and social change—at least, explanations deeper than those now offered on the social and cultural levels—must take account of biological, psychological, and physical factors. But problems of this kind are peripheral to present considerations. We are concerned with ascertaining the nature of the sociocultural systems at each different level of organization.

According to the principle of sociocultural sublevels, each higher sublevel is more complex than the lower ones not only in the qualitative sense that it has more parts but, as in biological sublevels, that it has qualitatively novel characteristics or unique properties which are not evident in or foreshadowed by the lower ones. That is, the new whole at each higher sublevel induces changes in the very nature of the parts and creates new relationships between the parts and to the whole.

This point may be illustrated with a simple and basic phenomenon. The human family is found in all societies but, like the cell, its nature and functions vary according to the whole. In a few sociocultural units, such as the Eskimo or the Great Basin Shoshoneans, the family more or less constitutes the social, economic, educational, and political whole. The family has persisted throughout world history, but its nature and role in larger sociocultural wholes have changed tremendously. The contemporary American family, for example, has lost many of the primitive functions, while others have been so modified as to give it unique meaning and relationships that are specific to the context of modern civilization.

In the historical development of sociocultural systems, the individual family units amalgamated into larger groups whose nature and functions were very different from those of the family. There are and have been many kinds of primitive multifamily societies, each representing an integrated whole. One variety of multifamily local group is that found in aboriginal Yucatan. The native Maya states collapsed after the Spanish

Conquest, and a high degree of local separatism was established among the Indian groups. Gradually and in varying degrees these people were brought under the influence of Merida, a city of the European pattern. Redfield, speaking of Yucatan, characterizes the folk society [10] as small, isolated, close-knit, homogeneous, simple in technology, patterned around kinship relations, having implicit goals and values, and believing in all-pervading supernaturalism. In Yucatan, under the influence of urban or national culture,[11] the many collectivized folk activities became individualized, the all-pervasive supernaturalism receded, much of life became secularized, and the close-knit folk society was disorganized. But the changes in the folk society and folk culture of Yucatan could also be described in terms of their readaptation to a new and higher level of sociocultural organization. From the point of view of the folk society, the individual's life became secularized, individualized, and disorganized. From the point of view of the larger whole or the newer pattern, scientific or naturalistic explanations replaced supernatural ones in many spheres of life; the organized church partly replaced informal, local religious outlets; affiliations with the kin group and the local group were partly superseded by affiliations with urban (or national) occupational, social class, and other special groups; and when the individual ceased to be one of many similar individuals who cooperated in a local homogeneous whole, he assumed a specialized role in a larger heterogeneous system. Folk societies and cultures do not entirely disappear but they are modified and acquire new characteristics because of their functional dependence upon a new and larger system.

These remarks on the transformations in a folk society when it is absorbed into a larger sociocultural unit are intended merely to illustrate the modifications in functions of the former.

[10] Robert Redfield, "The Folk Society," *American Journal of Sociology*, 52: 293–308 (1947).
[11] Robert Redfield, *The Folk Culture of Yucatan*.

It is purely a matter of definition whether the folk society is said to disappear when it becomes a dependent part of a larger organizational whole—and there are many definitions and concepts of "folk society."

The concept of sociocultural levels, of course, implies a developmental continuum, but the question of where to draw the lines between levels—that of a developmental taxonomy—must be answered on a comparative empirical basis if the organizational wholes are to be conceptualized in such a way as to facilitate a problem approach in research. Sociological taxonomy has tended to be so logical and abstract as to have little bearing on reality. For example, Sorokin's classification of social groups into families, clans, tribes ("an organized and solidary agglomeration of two or more clans"!), and nations [12] is not based on empirical cross-cultural studies, for few such studies have been made. There are unquestionably typological similarities between societies of the differing cultural traditions represented in the major world areas, but considerable comparative study will be necessary to isolate recurrent dynamics of developmental process and of structural-functional types.

On primitive levels, "family," "clan," and "tribe" are largely unreal concepts. Many primitive peoples never had clans, and "tribe" has a great many meanings. The social typology of primitive peoples is exceedingly complex and has largely to be worked out. One type that has been established cross-culturally is the "patrilineal band," an extended, exogamous, land-owning patrilineal kin group which is found among Australians, Bushmen, Fuegians, Southern California Shoshoneans, and certain other primitive hunters.[13] This is but one of many types of primitive bands, each with its own ecological adaptations, social structure, and functional relations.

[12] Sorokin, *op. cit.*, pp. 251–255.
[13] Julian H. Steward, "The Economic and Social Basis of Primitive Bands," in *Essays in Anthropology Presented to A. L. Kroeber* (Berkeley: University of California Press, 1936), pp. 331–350.

The "folk society" is at present a highly abstract construct—almost a definition—rather than a type based on cross-cultural data. Redfield's particular concept of folk society and his statement of the effects of urbanizing influences on it apply specifically to Yucatan. He offers these as hypotheses for cross-cultural testing and not as validated universals. In the different world areas there are hundreds of societies which might be considered "folk" from one point of view or another. For research, the concept of "folk" needs to be concretized in terms of actual sociocultural groups. If certain types are found in several different areas, the concept has operational utility in developmental and functional studies. Setting up a type as a logical construct rather than as an abstraction of forms which occur in concrete situations is likely to have limited use.

Similarly, "nation" is too broad a concept to have much significance, for dozens of wholly unlike societies in the ancient and modern world might loosely be defined as nations. Wittfogel's "oriental absolute state" is a type established cross-culturally on the basis of empirical data. This concept has operational utility because it relates a particular social, political, and economic structure to particular kinds of natural environment and land use in several centers of ancient civilizations.[14]

More realistic types in sociological taxonomy are modern nations, particularly those of the Western world, for they have been extensively studied. It does not follow, however, that nations in other world areas can be approached by use of the concepts developed with reference to these Western nations, because the structure, functions, and values of the former differ from those of the latter. Above all, it is utterly fallacious to conceive of any developmental continuum of social types as representing a sequence of stages through which all mankind passed. Universal developmental stages, such as those postulated by L. H. Morgan, have long since been rejected. Whatever

[14] K. A. Wittfogel, "The Foundations and Stages of Chinese Economic History," *Zeitschrift für Sozialforschung*, 4:26–60 (1935).

mankind may have in common has to be ascertained by the long and tedious process of detailed comparisons of society with society and area with area. It cannot be achieved by any deductive process.

If a developmental and structural-functional taxonomy is to be useful in studying such problems as the growth of nationalism, economic development, impact of industrialized nations on backward peoples, spread of political ideologies, and other themes of interest, it is necessary first to understand sociocultural units in their particular relativistic area settings before abstracting out structural features or developmental processes that are common to societies in two or more areas.

The concepts of level of organization and of developmental continuum indicate the need of recognizing that in each world area the sequences of sociocultural units consist of successions of new kinds of wholes qualitatively different from previous ones but genetically related to them. Where to draw the lines between levels should depend more upon the particular problem under investigation than on any a priori logical construct. Each sociocultural system can provide the frame of reference within which interdisciplinary data are integrated; but the nature and method of integration will depend upon the level or kind of organization. The higher, more complex levels will require contributions from many more specialized disciplines.

Sociocultural Systems as Research Units

In this section some research implications of the concept of levels of sociocultural systems will be suggested, but no attempt will be made to prescribe any universal methodology. The general theme of interest, the research problem, and the nature of the unit of study determine the methodology appropriate to each project.

Among most primitive peoples the localized unit is the sociocultural whole; the society is small and self-contained and the culture is fairly simple. The ethnographic method can usually be applied by one person since it is comparatively easy to study the functional interrelationship of all aspects of behavior in small independent societies.

As societies become more complex, special social groups begin to cut across local societies, and formal national institutions begin to appear. The whole consists of three kinds of parts: (1) the local units, such as communities, neighborhoods, households, and other special groups, which may be called vertical divisions of the larger whole; (2) special occupational, class, caste, racial, ethnic, or other subsocieties which, like the local units, may have a somewhat distinctive way of life, but which cut across localities and may be called horizontal sociocultural segments; and (3) the formal institutions, such as money, banking, trade, legal systems, education, militarism, organized churches, philosophical and political ideologies, and the like, which constitute the bones, nerves, and sinews running throughout the total society, binding it together, and affecting it at every point. The vertical and horizontal sociocultural subgroups make up the total social structure. The institutions as such usually do not constitute sociocultural segments, although they affect and are affected by all segments.

As societies develop to higher levels of organization, the horizontal sociocultural segments and the formal institutions attain increasing importance. In contemporary civilizations they are so important that the institutions have become the specialties of different disciplines. The means of interrelating these fields of specialization in modern area research, however, are not yet clear.

The local units or communities, as we have seen, are treated by many anthropologists and sociologists as if they were independent, self-sufficient, sociocultural systems. Their place in the larger structure is rarely clarified, and the effect of national institutions upon them receives little attention. The methodology for understanding the community in its larger context must be adapted to the particular case. Tarascan communities retain a great deal of folk culture; they have fewer horizontal sociocultural segments and are less affected by national institutions than Middletown in the United States.

The horizontal segments are generally studied with reference to a total social structure and are identified by such basic criteria as income, social status, and occupation. There has been virtually no application of the ethnographic method to these segments comparable to its use in community studies. Responses to questionnaires, designed primarily to yield quantitative data, have shown some of the outstanding characteristics of horizontal segments. The ethnographic method should also be used in study of these segments, for it is probable that many of them have subcultures just as communities do. It is even possible that in a nation like the United States, the horizontal segments often represent the more important subcultural divisions, which in many cases have a degree of organization. Whereas a Tarascan individual is primarily attached to his family, neighborhood, or community in which even the church, school, and political organizations have more local than national significance, many Americans have few ties with their localities. They may hardly know their immediate neighbors; they may or may not participate in the local Parent-Teachers Association, American Legion, or other organizations; and their principal interests and connections may lie entirely outside the community. They may belong to labor unions, the National Association of Manufacturers, scientific or professional societies, churches, lodges, or other organizations and institutions which ally them more closely functionally with people scattered throughout the nation than with the person next door.

It is probable that there are many interlocality horizontal segments which have true subcultures, and these would be well worth studying. There are indications of such subcultures in certain community studies. For example, the laboring class and the middle-class businessmen of Middletown are culturally different, but does each resemble its own class in other communities? Novelists like Sinclair Lewis are still the principal authority for the hypothesis that middle-class businessmen have about the same culture everywhere. Social science might well set itself the task of investigating this hypothesis.

The formal institutions of the more complex societies are the concern of many special disciplines—economics, government, law, history, literature, philosophy, and others. As most of these developed in the study of Euro-American societies, the concepts of culture, cultural relativity, and sociocultural systems are only now beginning to be used in them. Until recently they were becoming more and more specialized and compartmentalized. Theoretically it should be possible to make as completely integrated an interdisciplinary study of the United States as of a primitive tribe. Practically this will be impossible as long as specialized studies, which will always be necessary, are not more closely coordinated. Just how this will be brought about is not clear, but some of the major themes of interest previously mentioned probably will lead to interdisciplinary studies. Whether the themes are conceived as relating to practical problems or to scientific interests does not matter. Research will be so planned that it will cut across disciplinary lines. Adequate conceptualization of the nature of the sociocultural whole and its parts in each case will indicate the relevance of different fields of specialization to any interdisciplinary approach to the basic themes of interest.

Cross-cultural Problems and Methods

Previous sections have stressed the importance of problems in area research, of which the scientific goal is to develop a method which will make social and cultural prediction possible. Prediction, however, may be understood differently. By the principle of cultural relativity, which in its extreme sense implies that no two world areas are alike, prediction would mean that the people of any area can be expected to behave "in character" and the task would be to ascertain the cultural particulars which determine their behavior. This principle, however, seems to preclude the possibility of making predictive formulations which are valid for two or more areas. Such formulations would have to be made in terms of recurrent cause and effect, but the extreme relativists see any culture as a unique entity in which all the phenomena are so interdependent that each is both cause and effect.

The problem approach to area research, however, generally implies that certain general trends may be found in the area particulars. For example, the impact of industrial nations upon backward areas has some common characteristics. Emergent nationalism has similar aspects in different parts of the world. The search for general laws is an ideal of many area research workers.

A. V. Kidder, in a mimeographed account of the Carnegie Institution's Maya program, states that:

> The question . . . is: does culture, although not biologically transmitted, develop and function in response to tendencies—it is perhaps too connotative to call them law—that are comparable to those controlling biological evolution? There seems to be evidence that, in some degree at least, it does. All over the world and among populations that could apparently not possibly have come into contact with each other, similar inventions have been made and have been made in a seemingly predetermined order. Extraordinary similarities are to be observed in the nature and order of appearance among widely separated peoples of certain social practices and religious observances.
>
> These are likenesses, not identities; history, to reverse the proverb, never repeats itself; different environments and differing opportunities have seen to that. But they do seem to indicate that there are definite tendencies and orderlinesses, both in the growth of this compelling force and in man's responses thereto. It is therefore the task of the disciplines concerned with man and his culture—genetics, history, archaeology, sociology, the humanities—to gather and to correlate information which may enable us more fully to understand these now dimly perceived trends and relationships.

The search for laws or universals has been notably lacking in a comparative cross-cultural approach.[15] Too often the formulations concerning function or process that result from the analysis of a single society are postulated as universal laws. As long as these are not tested in other societies, they are no more than hypotheses and may be no more than descriptions of particular characteristics of our own Western European culture. Such "laws" as those concerning the behavior of money, the profit motive, or business cycles may not at all be valid for other societies, except as the latter have been drawn into the orbit of Western capitalism, and even in these cases the "laws" may require drastic modification. Characteristics of the family which are correlated with income or social status may apply only to Western civilization. Assumptions about political behavior, such as those which presumably underlie public opinion polling methods, would certainly not be applicable elsewhere—and apparently require some modification to be reliable in our own rapidly changing society.

Fei and Chang[16] have given an interesting illustration of how assumptions about American land use and land tenure cannot be directly transferred to China. They criticize Buck's[17] questionnaire approach to land use in China on the grounds that, "following the American convention, villagers are classified into landowner, part owner, tenant, landless laborers, and nonfarming villagers." They point out that a better understanding of the local variations of Chinese society would show that tenants in Yunnan may work the land of collective clan owners and thus be in a very different social and economic position than are tenants in Kiangsu who rent from absentee landlords, and

---

[15] This point has been discussed by the writer and its application illustrated in "Cultural Causality and Law: A Trial Formulation of the Development of Early Civilizations," *op. cit.*

[16] *Earthbound China, op. cit.*, pp. 2–4.

[17] John L. Buck, *Land Utilization in China* (Chicago: University of Chicago Press, 1937).

again that hired labor in some areas may be migratory, not resident.

A serious obstacle to an approach to cross-cultural laws or regularities is the evident belief that a law, whether of developmental processes or stages or of functional dynamics, must apply to all mankind. The objective is usually phrased as the search for "universals." In the article cited,[18] the writer endeavored to show that the immediate aim should be to formulate cause and effect relationships, whether of a synchronic or diachronic nature, that pertain to delimitable and specifiable conditions and situations rather than to seek universals. Many formulations may be valid for two or more areas, but the varieties of world cultures, past and present, differ so greatly because of both area tradition and sociocultural level that it can hardly be expected that formulations will hold for all mankind. And there is not the slightest need that they should.

The study of patrilineal bands [19] is a simple illustration of the procedure in a cross-cultural formulation of cause and effect. The problem was to ascertain what cultural-ecological factors contributed to the formation of certain kinds of exogamous hunting and gathering bands. Relevant phenomena included natural landscape, the nature and distribution of wild game, hunting technology, population density, patterns of kinship and exogamy, and relative status of men and women in the culture. It was found that the adjustment of man to nature—cultural ecology—under particular conditions brought about bands that were patrilineal, exogamous, patrilocal, and land-owning. These features represent an independently recurrent type which is an abstraction of similarities, although the total culture of each band consists of innumerable particulars which in their totality are unique.

The method of abstracting recurrent functional interrela-

[18] "Cultural Causality and Law."
[19] Julian H. Steward, "The Economic and Social Basis of Primitive Bands," *op. cit.*

tionships in higher sociocultural levels is essentially the same, although its application is far more difficult because the phenomena are not only more complex and qualitatively different than in simpler societies but their study has been divided among different disciplines.

Formulations that pertain to a complex society may be illustrated by hypotheses which were developed by the staff of the Puerto Rico project. Had the purpose of this project been to describe the culture according to the concept of the culture area, the task would have been simply to list those cultural features which comprise the common denominator of the Island, those which it shares with the larger Ibero-American culture area, and those which it shares with the United States. But there are many patterns and processes of land use, land tenure, colonialism, economic and political dependency, nationalism, and other matters which are not limited to Puerto Rico. Each can be stated as a hypothesis of the causal relationships that may be expected under stipulated circumstances. Applied to Puerto Rico, it was necessary to specify the particular characteristics of the Island that were related to the hypothesis and to look to different discipline for relevant data.

Initially the hypotheses were derived from discussions in a seminar at Columbia University and from readings of the staff. At first one could not be certain whether each formulation was merely descriptive of Puerto Rico's Ibero-American heritage or whether it represented function and process that occur anywhere under designated conditions. The problems or hypotheses therefore had to be stated as pertaining to specifiable conditions. The Island's Spanish heritage originally included an agrarian two-class (landlord and peasant) society, concentration of power in the land owners, and a strong church sanction of the system, the church and state being almost inseparable; and it still includes such features as the Spanish language, towns which are built around plazas, patrilineal families, close familial ties, and a dual standard. Puerto Rico, like every other Latin

American nation, also developed special characteristics of its own and it acquired various features from the United States. Consequently any hypothesis about Puerto Rico which might be valid cross-culturally would have to abstract general features from Puerto Rico's particular cultural heritage. If a hypothesis pertained to Puerto Rico's unique characteristics, it would by definition obtain nowhere else. On the other hand, any hypothesis that might be true for all mankind would probably be so broad as to lack real significance. Between these extremes are hypotheses pertaining to conditions that are generalized in varying degrees. For example, hypotheses might pertain to any agrarian society, to any colonial dependency, or to any colonial dependency of a capitalist society.

A very broad, though not universal, hypothesis might be: "In any agricultural society, children are a nonsalaried essential of the labor force." A more limited hypothesis would be: "In any capitalist society, if high male unemployment and seasonal work reduce the relative importance of the male's contribution, woman's authority in the family and society increases; the concentration of productive resources in the hands of one class continues progressively; consumption on credit varies from class to class; power is exercised by higher leaders and delegated to local leaders, rather than the reverse; the lines of political power correspond to the lines of economic power; the production of subsistence commodities progressively diminishes while production for the world market increases; and there is an observable concentration of land ownership in fewer and fewer hands."

For the purpose of cross-cultural comparison and formulation of hypotheses of a more specific nature, some of the basic characteristics of Puerto Rico are: agrarian, dependent upon cash, credit, and industrially manufactured goods; capitalistic, with private ownership of lands and other means of production, and a system of power and social status. To limit the conditions further, Puerto Rico is insular, tropical, and a dependency of the United States after having been a colony of Spain. Conditions could obviously be narrowed to the point where they pertained to Puerto Rico alone and had no cross-cultural validity. It is incumbent upon anyone seeking cultural regularities to designate the point that separates the particulars of a cultural heritage from those features which are more general.

The requirement that a formulation of regularities interrelate as many phenomena as seem to have casual connection may be illustrated by another hypothesis which may have wide cross-cultural applicability: "An agrarian society which is part of a capitalist economy of which class structure is a characteristic, which has access to manufactured goods, and which produces predominantly cash crops, will have individual landownership, bilateral inheritance, and competition for markets; the small owner will be at a disadvantage because of lack of credit and relatively greater overhead expenses; and because lands are split among heirs, the ever-decreasing size of the holdings of small owners will reach the point where the owners cannot compete with the large owners and therefore will lose their lands to them." A corollary hypothesis is: "Two basic types of economy, such as capitalist and cooperative, cannot coexist in any society. Therefore, government intervention or other means of reversing the trend just stated can be applied only to a very limited extent; for power resides in the landowners, who could stop the contrary trend if it began to threaten them."

Another hypothetical formulation of regularities, which interrelates a considerable number of cultural features while pertaining to delimitable conditions, concerns the correlates of large and small farms. It is drawn from previous research, especially from Arensberg and Kimball's Irish study: "In a capitalist industrial society, large and small farmers will differ in a number of ways that are causally interrelated and self-consistent. The larger farmer will have specialized cash crops; purchase many essential foods and material goods; have greater credit, smaller overhead, and greater mechanization; make more extensive use of fertilizers and other scientific methods, these deriving in part from his capital available to employ such aids and in part from his greater education and wider contacts. The large owner will belong to the middle or upper class, and thereby participate to a greater degree in the national culture. His laborers will work for wages, purchase more of their needs, have small bilateral family units, and lack cooperation because there are no activities for cooperation. (Here could be included trends toward unionization, etc., although these would have to be postulated with reference to more specific circumstances.)

"The small farmer will grow more general produce, including subsistence crops, and correspondingly he will have less cash income for the purchase of manufactured goods. For this reason homecrafts will supply a portion of his material needs that varies in direct ratio to the portion of his production that brings a cash income. His farming will be less mechanized. It will entail more mutual help, between both relatives and neighbors. Family ties will be more extended. Village cohesion will be greater, being based not only on economic cooperation but on common religious, political, and social interests. Whereas the hired laborer of the large farm is of the lower class, that is, the national proletariat, the small farmer is more independent of the national structure and more locally distinctive in culture, not falling so readily into a class system and not participating in the national system of credit, trade, education, and intellectual and esthetic values."

These hypotheses may apply to total sociocultural wholes or to special parts or aspects of wholes. They illustrate the kinds of formulations which may be made in any study and tested in other studies. They will be applicable only to stipulated conditions. Both the hypotheses and the conditions will doubtless need to be reformulated as they are tested cross-culturally.

Virtually all important area problems can be converted into hypotheses for cross-cultural testing, and these hypotheses can orient research. Historical-cultural particularism is essentially factualism, and it provides no criteria nor frame of reference by which to judge the relevance of data. If, however, the more general purpose of social science is to ascertain the regularities, the laws, or the causes and effects in human behavior, specific formulations of postulated regularities must necessarily guide the selection of research problems and of relevant data.

The conditions of the problem approach are that the postulated regularities be so phrased as to: (1) distinguish general and recurrent factors involved in cause and effect relationships from locally distinctive particulars of the cultural heritage; (2) be subject to cross-cultural validation; (3) specify the conditions to which they pertain; and (4) interrelate all pertinent phenomena.

Social science literature is filled with suggestions of regularities that may be cross-culturally valid. The present need is to make the implied hypotheses explicit and to subject them to empirical test.

CHAPTER IV

THEORY AND PRACTICE OF AN AREA APPROACH: THE PUERTO RICO PROJECT

The preceding chapters have attempted to conceptualize area units in such a way that they could serve as frames of reference for an interdisciplinary approach, to specify some of the terms for integration of the data produced by the different disciplines studying a particular area, and to indicate that focus upon a problem is essential to any fruitful area program. It was concluded that for research purposes the area unit must be conceived as a sociocultural system or whole, that is, as a structural entity consisting of many kinds of sociocultural segments or subgroups and of institutions which are in a functional or dependency relationship to one another and to the whole. These segments and institutions have long been the special concern of different disciplines. An interdisciplinary approach that seeks integration in area terms must formulate research problems that involve the interrelationship of phenomena in terms of the area whole.

The Puerto Rico project was designed to study the social anthropology of the Island. Its initial orientation was anthropological. It was recognized that many kinds of information necessary to the principal task must come from disciplines other than anthropology, but exactly what this information was and how it related to anthropological studies was not clear until the project had been in operation for many months. If we had to repeat the project, we would include a psychologist, economist, sociologist, agronomist, and perhaps other specialists from the beginning. Insofar as other areas are similar to Puerto Rico, this project may suggest problems and methods for interdisciplinary cooperation elsewhere.

The methodological conclusions to be drawn from the Puerto Rico project do not of course apply to all areas. The concept of different levels of sociocultural organization means that particular problems and methods are applicable only to types of areas sharing specifiable characteristics. A single anthropologist can study an Australian tribe; a large number of specialists have been working for years on contemporary Euro-American nations. Most contemporary area studies are concerned either with modern civilizations of different kinds or with folk cultures and societies that have come under some form of Euro-American or Russian dominance. All these studies consequently involve very complex sociocultural units, which have institutions that extend far beyond the geographical, political, and even cultural limits of the peoples or societies being investigated.

The central problem of the Puerto Rico project stemmed from anthropology but it must be stressed that the kind of interdisciplinary cooperation used was by no means the only kind which might have been used. Problems originating in the interests of other disciplines may require different approaches. It is difficult, however, to see how the conceptualization of Puerto Rico as an area whole can be very different from the point of view of other disciplines. If the present conceptualization stands, then it may provide a framework into which any approach fits. That is, all studies will contribute to a gradual understanding of the Island as an entity with respect to both its internal structure and function and its external relations.

The Problem and Objectives [1]

Because the method of social anthropology is to analyze all aspects of a culture and ascertain how they are functionally

[1] The Puerto Rico project was suggested and sponsored by the Social Science Research Center of the University of Puerto Rico, which was then under the direction of Clarence Senior, and during the project under that of Simon Rottenberg. It was financed in about equal amounts by the University of Puerto Rico

interrelated, study of the social anthropology of Puerto Rico seemed an impossible objective. Puerto Rico is a highly complex entity, which had already been studied extensively, though not completely, by many specialists. Puerto Rico had also been described as a whole in various publications, but there were large gaps in information necessary to understanding it as a whole. One of the greatest needs was to know more about the major variations in the culture or way of life of the rural population. Only four brief community studies had been made: three by sociologists—Charles Rogler, Rafael Pico, and Caroline Ware, and one by an anthropologist, Morris Siegel.

Whereas the first need that anthropology could meet was a

---

and by the Rockefeller Foundation, and ran from February 1948 through August 1949.

John Murra of the University of Puerto Rico served as field director during the first phase of the work, which was devoted to community studies. Subsequently, because of Professor Murra's heavy teaching obligations, the writer assumed active directorship in the second phase, which was devoted to comparative studies of community phenomena and to the role of formal institutions as integrating factors in the insular whole and as factors of change.

The chief personnel of the project consisted of four advanced students from the Department of Anthropology at Columbia University, Raymond Scheele, Sidney Mintz, Robert Manners, and Eric Wolf, the last two accompanied by their wives who assisted actively in the field work, and one advanced student in anthropology from the University of Chicago, Elena Padilla. Isabel Caro of the University of Chicago joined the project later, but was forced to return to the United States because of illness in her family. Robert Armstrong, also of the University of Chicago and visiting professor at the University of Puerto Rico, participated in the project so far as time permitted. Four Puerto Ricans, Angelina Roca, Charles Rosario, Delia Ortega, and Edwin Seda, cooperated with the Americans.

The administration of the project, although formerly determined by the advisory committee and the director, was actually in the hands of the field workers. The principle underlying this was that when responsible and competent personnel has accepted the obligations of a project it should not be coerced, for individual scholarship requires intellectual freedom. The belief of many persons that scholars are so extremely individualistic that they cannot work together as a team was certainly not supported in this case. Having joined the project because of interest in the problem, the members submerged individual differences and gave unanimous support to decisions reached by a majority of the staff. The role of the advisory committee and the directors ordinarily was to advise and persuade rather than to dictate.

study of the rural population, knowledge of it would be quite incomplete if the project did no more than record variations in community and regional subcultures. These subcultures had to be seen as parts of an insular whole, subject to influence by the various institutions studied by other disciplines, and the Island as a whole had to be seen in relationship to other areas, especially the United States. Thus any local data had to be related to the larger facts, and conclusions had to be stated as pertaining to a situation with specifiable characteristics.

Puerto Rico has certain general characteristics that make it a fairly definite sociocultural type and that dictated the general problem and methods of the project. It has a cultural heritage that is predominantly Hispanic, showing little evidence of either native Indian or African culture, but its 2,200,000 people show a racial mixture of white, Negro, and Indian. It is fairly small, insular, and subtropical. It has long been colonial, first under Spain, and during the last 50 years under the United States. It is agrarian, rural, and economically part of a capitalist world in that it depends upon an export crop and imports nearly all its manufactured goods and about half its food.

Although the principal task was anthropological study of the rural cultures, every effort was made to enlist the cooperation of other disciplines and to use their data. The final achievement in the direction of integrating all social science data in terms of the Island whole will of course be relative. Anthropologists cannot do this alone, and much information of many kinds is needed. The final synthesis of the results of the project, therefore, will represent a conceptualization of the whole as a special kind of sociocultural system and use of interdisciplinary data to explain the main cultural variations of the Island. It will by no means be a final interpretation of the Island.

BACKGROUND KNOWLEDGE FOR AREA RESEARCH

For any research program dealing with the culture of an area or with some special sociocultural unit within it, the research workers must be equipped with as much basic knowledge of the area as possible. They must have knowledge, first, of the fundamental institutions, such as the basic production and relationship of the area to world trade and economics, the legal system, the formal political organization, the political ideology and related philosophy and cultural values, the religious organization and doctrines, the total social structure, and the educational system. Second, they must be familiar with the results of previous cultural studies or sociological surveys of sociocultural segments, such as communities, ethnic or racial minorities, or social classes. Third, they must have a working knowledge of the language not only because it is an essential research tool, but also because the native literature is a rich source of information and because language per se affords many insights into cultural attitudes and values. Fourth, they should have knowledge of the cultural history, that is, the development of the principal cultural institutions.

Without such knowledge, research time will be lost and wrong conclusions may be reached. A social scientist experienced in his own society might carry an ethnocentric view to the field, unaware that his basic concepts about economic or political phenomena might not be true of a culture other than his own. He might study the ethnography of a community in ignorance of the national legal system, the political ideologies, the religious and philosophical concepts, the economic motivations, or the educational goals which all the communities share with the larger society. Current area training programs have the enormous value to research of supplying much of this background information.

As Columbia University has no Latin American Institute, the Puerto Rico project undertook to meet this need in two ways:

(1) Eight months before the field work was started, a survey of historical sources was begun. This survey abstracted data on the cultural origins of Puerto Rico, and especially the effects of Puerto Rico's changing colonial status and the economic

basis of its social and cultural patterns. The sources afford meager information on the local or folk culture, but they do reveal the general economic, political, and social trends that have originated largely outside the Island and that are basic to the present situation.

(2) Just prior to initiation of the project, a one-semester seminar at Columbia University was devoted to a review of the social science literature concerning the Island. In a sense this seminar was a sequel to one given the previous year, devoted to a survey and analysis of the principal anthropological studies of contemporary communities and minority groups in different parts of the world. (The section of Chapter II analyzing community studies is partly based on the results of this seminar.) The conceptual and methodological insights gained in the earlier seminar were to be applied in the field work, particular stress being laid on problems and methods reported in monographs on communities in other parts of the world.

The Puerto Rico seminar included all field workers, except those from the University of Chicago and the University of Puerto Rico, who later joined the field staff. The subjects reported on by the seminar members were cultural history, demography and statistics, the sugar industry, other economic activities, United States policies, social structure, race relations, and ideologies. In addition, Frank Tannenbaum described rural workers and Kingsley Davis discussed the sociological survey that he and Paul Hatt were carrying out.

This background coverage was as good as could be managed under the circumstances. A multidisciplinary coverage of Latin America in an area program would have helped enormously. Even such a program, however, would necessarily have been unable to give a very good picture of Spanish culture as a whole, especially that of the colonial period, because the necessary studies of sixteenth century Spain, Spanish archives, and Hispanic cultures in different parts of the world have not been made. In Puerto Rico, a knowledge of the early Spanish heritage would have been of great assistance in distinguishing those features which are specific to this heritage from those which are the inevitable result of colonialism, agrarianism, dependence upon an export crop, and so forth, and which may be postulated to develop in any culture where these factors are present.

FIELD STUDIES

The field work was planned to consist of three phases: (1) a survey of the Island and selection of communities; (2) the community studies; (3) analysis of the relation of the communities to one another and to the insular whole. The three phases were closely interrelated as the first and second made provision for periodic meetings of the entire staff, not only to discuss problems and methods of general interest but to consult with specialists on different subjects as the occasion required, while the third phase allowed for return visits to the communities to check information and to obtain data which the consultations showed to be important after consideration of broader problems. The third phase of the work naturally took the anthropologists considerably beyond their ordinary skills and knowledge. Inadequate as the final picture of the insular whole may be, however, there is no doubt that the efforts to relate the community studies to this larger whole will have made these studies infinitely better than they would have been if approached only in terms of themselves according to traditional methods.

In the traditional approach, as already pointed out (pp. 44–45), a community is all too often selected on the basis of its size, accessibility, convenience, charm, or some other often trivial characteristic rather than for its theoretical importance. Also, it has usually been studied as if it were a primitive tribe, all aspects of its culture being described according to an ideal outline or inventory rather than in terms of definite problems.

When communities have been selected in a larger, more theoretical frame of reference and studied with definite problems in mind, the findings inevitably have had greater meaning and wider applicability. The studies of Ireland by Arensberg and Kimball, of Yucatan by Redfield and his colleagues, of Middletown by the Lynds, of China by Fei and his associates, and of Japan by Embree were particularly stimulating to the Puerto Rico project.

The members of the Puerto Rico project spent considerable time both before and after arriving on the Island considering the theory of community selection and choosing communities for study.

Theoretical Basis of Community Selection

As Puerto Rico is overwhelmingly agrarian and rural, our chief task was to study the way of life of its farm population. We wished the studies to be representative of as large a portion of the Island's 2,200,000 people as possible. A second task, which grew out of the endeavor to understand the Island as a whole rather than merely as a composite of communities and farm regions, was to study the culture, and the social, political, and economic role of the metropolitan upper classes.

The farm communities were chosen on the basis of certain theoretical assumptions. Principally it was assumed that, while the broad patterns of Puerto Rican life were determined by the Hispanic heritage and by the colonial position and subtropical nature of the Island, regional cultural differences resulted from adaptations of the productive complexes, that is, land use, to different local environments. Such a hypothesis seemed inevitable because Puerto Rico's cultural heritage and its cultural contacts with both Spain and the United States have been constants; neither could explain local variations. The very great local differences could be explained only by cultural-ecological processes—the processes by which production, social patterns, and related modes of life are selectively borrowed from outside sources and adapted to local needs in each natural region. More concretely it was suspected that, despite the Island's common cultural background and extra-insular contacts, the way of life in the coffee area, the tobacco and mixed crops area, and in the several sugar areas would differ profoundly. If so, the general assumption of cultural homogeneity that seems to have been the basis of the quantitative survey techniques used in many previous studies of Puerto Rico would have given only insular averages and failed to indicate the regional differences, which are no less important than the similarities. If circumstances permitted the study of only a single community, it would have to be selected as representing the Island in microcosm. Siegel and others had done this pioneering task. Our task was to investigate the variations and to explain them. Our field work has shown that cultural regionalism is very important in Puerto Rico.

As an initial indication of local variations, the project could use only productive processes—land use, land ownership, and a few related phenomena—which were known through previous surveys. The variations in the way of life that are corollaries of these processes were to be the subject of study and were still unknown.

Method of Community Selection

Several methods were used to choose communities that were representative of the different regions. The staff collaborated in the selection of communities.

First, to ascertain basic differences in production, all relevant census data and statistics were studied. Arensberg and Kimball had used census data in their study of Ireland to establish the fact that there were distinctive differences between large and small farmers, and they made the culture of the small farmers their object of study. In Puerto Rico census and other statistical materials were supplemented with data obtained from background literature and from local sources. Statistical data show that Puerto Rico's overwhelmingly important export crop is sugar. Tobacco and coffee were once important export crops also but both have largely lost their outside markets. Tobacco is now merely the most important of a considerable number of crops grown in portions of the interior (10 percent of production is in tobacco), while coffee is still predominantly a single crop throughout a large region. In estimating the importance of the different crops, statistics on production and proportion of the total land devoted to their cultivation were used.

Second, to obtain data on land ownership, it was necessary to supplement statistical information with field surveys. Data from the U.S. Census Bureau, the Agricultural Adjustment Administration, other federal and insular agencies, and local (municipio) listings were used. These materials are ordinarily not broken down by communities. Consequently, each field worker visited a region which has a distinctive type of production and made a preliminary survey to obtain further information on land ownership and related features. He consulted municipio mayors, labor union leaders, school directors, and other authorities, political committeemen, farm foremen and overseers, farm owners, tenant farmers, and wage earners. These persons provided valuable qualitative summaries of the conditions of life in their communities, and in some cases they helped correct out-of-date statistics. It was found that ownership of land is by private individuals in the regions of coffee and of tobacco and mixed crops; and while there is a considerable range in the size of holdings, medium-sized farms seemed to be most typical. The same is true of only a small portion of the sugar region, most sugar production being in very large holdings, some of them corporate-owned and others government-owned. An additional factor in regional variation is share cropping and tenancy in the coffee and tobacco areas.

Third, after regions which represented the more important types of land use and land ownership had been selected, the final choice of one community for intensive study, from among several typical communities, was based on additional considerations—size (it had to be small enough for a team of two persons, a North American and a Puerto Rican, to handle) and other factors.

Now that the community studies are completed, it is believed that the choices were justified in terms of the original problems.

Were other communities to be studied in the future, there are additional types which could profitably be investigated, although they represent numerically small portions of the Island population, and in some instances they involve problems other than the basic one of cultural ecological processes in relation to local differentiation. A community representing a transition from one type of farming to another would throw light on cultural processes, and the project had hoped to study a community in an intermediate stage of giving up coffee production for sugar. Several communities engage in specialized production, for example, fishing, needlework, and dairy farming, but none of these involve great numbers of people. There are also communities which are supposed to preserve patterns of an older and generally outmoded way of life, some representing older Hispanic patterns and others, predominantly Negro in race, preserving a certain amount of African culture. These are atypical because, while they are important in terms of cultural processes, they do not represent significant numbers of the contemporary population and they have been least affected by influences from outside the Island, particularly from the United States. Furthermore, there is some doubt as to whether they are true survivals untouched by contemporary trends, and whether the processes of change may not be determined more readily by use of elderly informants, documents, municipal archives, and histories, than by attempting to disentangle the seemingly old from the new in these "traditional" communities.

Another purpose in community selection that was considered was the possibility of predicting future trends, especially where government planning is concerned. The community of government-operated sugar cane lands and grinding mills is perhaps a future potential for parts of the Island, and might profitably receive more attention from the point of view of planning. The process of urbanization clearly represents future trends, and a town was selected for partial study with this in mind. (In this case the research worker had too many duties at the University to continue this assignment.) In general, however, selections were directed toward obtaining an understanding of Puerto Rico as it is today and how it had become that way, rather than what it is likely to become. The project might also have chosen urban communities, such as San Juan, Caguas, or Ponce. Urbanization, however, is not yet typical of the Island, and an adequate study of any of the cities would have required the efforts of the entire field staff.

In some cases local attitudes and political factors suggested that field work in a community would be greatly handicapped.

The communities were chosen as localized sociocultural segments of society which were samples of the four or five principal regional variations. That is, each community and its surrounding farm area represented a loosely structured, somewhat self-contained functional segment of the Island. Were units of study to be selected in the United States, it is conceivable that such horizontal segments as farm laborers, middle-class professional groups, or certain types of industrial workers would be as significant for study as localized segments or communities. In Puerto Rico it was presumed that sociocultural segments had greater local than horizontal integration. At the same time most communities had several horizontal or class divisions and, in terms of the Island whole, these correspond to some extent from one region to another. This problem will be dealt with in the final synthesis of the insular whole.

Units of Study Selected

The following communities and sociocultural segments were finally selected for study: [2]

(1) A sugar-growing community on the south coast characterized by corporate ownership, large-scale irrigation, and mechanization. This community is typical of several south coast municipios and also of the culmination of a trend in national culture toward large absentee-ownership. Its population consists largely of laborers and resident managers, the older middle and upper classes having moved away.

(2) North coast communities where the government is the main owner of land and sugar mills, but where there is no irrigation and little mechanization. Like the south coast sugar communities, these consist largely of laborers, but there are several local variations: small resettlement communities; homesteads of 20 to 30 acres; and large, plantation-type profit sharing farms.

(3) A coffee-producing community in the western mountains. This municipio is characterized by traditional face-to-face relations between owners and workers, general lack of mechanization, concentration of land in the hands of Spanish-born owners, and considerable survival of old Hispanic patterns.

(4) A tobacco and mixed crops community in the central mountains. This region has privately owned farms, and most of them are small.

The study of these four types of communities has been as complete as possible in the time allowed. In addition, a study was begun of a sugar community on the northeast coast where the farms are of medium size and are operated by owners or tenants.

A special study was made of the upper class of the city of San Juan but this cannot be considered a community study

[2] Names of communities are not given, for it is believed that the social scientist has the obligation to protect his community and his informants from any repercussions that might result from full and candid reporting.

in the usual sense. The approach was cultural, however, in that it was designed to describe and analyze the culture or subculture of this group. As this class has very close connection with the United States, where its members spend considerable time, it was also regarded as a possible medium of transmission of American influence to the Island. Finally, its prominent members were given special attention because of their economic, social, and political power. In a sense the upper class of San Juan, although only a small part of Puerto Rico's principal city, really is Puerto Rico's upper class or at least a large portion of it, and a focus of much power within the Island.

Methods of Study

The communities were studied according to the usual ethnographic method in that all aspects of behavior were described and interrelated; some 40 categories serve as major headings for filing information. Field techniques included random and directed interviews, collection of case histories, participant observation, consultation of elderly informants, and use of archives, records, and other documents. As the application of qualitative anthropological methods to large and complex modern communities has been criticized on the grounds that the sampling is inadequate and the quantification insufficient, we devised a questionnaire which was given to a large number of persons. It was used at the end of the study, only after the qualitative methods had shown what questions were important and after the field workers were known in their communities and had had long experience in field work.

Use of the questionnaire was extremely successful, and we believe that the procedure of first acquiring a fairly explicit knowledge of the culture before a questionnaire is applied is to be recommended for three reasons: (1) It makes it possible to frame questions that will be meaningful in terms of known culture; (2) it helps establish local and class variations; and (3) it can be applied by trained field workers. In these respects its value is to quantify what is already known qualitatively. An alternative procedure which would seek to establish both qualitative and quantitative data for the entire Island in a single operation would almost inevitably fail to recognize the essential qualitative facts and variations, without which quantification is meaningless.

The project was able to investigate in the field a considerable number of problems which had been suggested by studies elsewhere. Among these were: variations from rural or folk society to urban society; a testing of the conventional three-class concept of social organization and devising of new concepts of class structure; race attitudes and race relations; and factors and trends in land tenure.

An historic approach was basic to the entire project. Each community was studied with special reference to changes since 1898, when Puerto Rico came under the control of the United States. But the history of all Hispanic and American institutions from the Conquest to 1948 will furnish a broad background to the development of the regional cultures.

The Insular or Area Whole

In considering Puerto Rico as a whole it was necessary to distinguish the concept of sociocultural unit from that of culture area. As a culture area Puerto Rico shares a Spanish heritage with Latin America, although it also has features borrowed from the United States. A list of the features which are common to all Puerto Ricans would not suggest structure and function. The Spanish language, for example, is a uniformity but it does not necessarily indicate a structural unity in Puerto Rico any more than it does in Latin America as a whole.

As a sociocultural unit Puerto Rico was considered to have two kinds of interdependent parts: (1) sociocultural subgroups or segments, which make up the total social structure; (2) formal institutions, which constitute the binding and regulating forces. The sociocultural segments consist of the localized societies or municipios, and the social, occupational, ethnic, and other special groups. The latter groups cut horizontally across communities and regions and, when arranged in hierarchical relationship, are known roughly as "classes." Such segments have distinctive subcultures and therefore fall within the legitimate scope of anthropology. The institutions, governmental, educational, economic, religious, and the like, do not in their formal aspects involve large cohesive groups of people with subcultures. Their organizational and technical intricacies have been the specialties of many disciplines.

To interrelate these parts in terms of a coherent insular whole, two steps were taken: (1) field data were compared to ascertain the principal sociocultural segments of the Island; (2) an interdisciplinary approach was used to relate these to the formal institutions. After the field work was completed, the staff met daily for a month to discuss differences between the regions and communities. Data were compared under the principal categories which had been used in the field. When the distinctive features of each community were related to one another from a functional point of view, it was evident that, despite the Island's common culture heritage and culture contacts, each community differed from the others in ways that could be explained by differences in environmental potentialities and in land use. Productive processes, land ownership, the family, marriage, social classes, religion, political attitudes, and even recreation formed parts of an integrated whole in each community.

Each community together with its dependent farm area represents a localized sociocultural segment. These segments are interrelated in several ways to make up the total insular social structure. First, there is some reciprocity between the regions in trade, especially of agricultural products, and in visiting and games. Second, the social classes into which the communities are divided extend to a certain degree from one community to another. The upper class, though small and somewhat localized in the cities, is wealthy and constitutes a socially exclusive in-group which has a superordinate position with respect to the entire Island. The other classes are less cohesive than the upper class but are by no means localized. Members of the professional classes are somewhat bound together by their professional activities and frequent association with one another. The laboring classes, especially the wage earners, have great horizontal mobility, being in fact forced to migrate where work is seasonal, and they tend to have the same reciprocal relationship to the higher classes. It is perhaps the small farm owners who have the fewest interregional ties.

The Island as a whole is regulated by a number of formal institutions: the legal and governmental system, few governmental functions being controlled locally; political parties; labor unions; the educational system; church organization and doctrine, both Catholic and Protestant; the army; certain organized sports; the distribution of cash crops and of manufactured goods and other commodities; and monetary systems, banking, and credit. It would be utterly presumptuous to suppose that anthropologists could deal adequately with the many technical and complicated aspects of these institutions. It was evident, however, that these constituted some of the principal binding forces of the Island and that they penetrated and profoundly affected every community. To have ignored them, consequently, would have left the community studies very incomplete.

In considering the best means of dealing with this problem, it was recognized that a distinction must be made between the formal institution and its local aspects or manifestations; for the latter are often very different from the former. For example, despite the formal Catholic doctrine, one community has a cult of saints while another has strong beliefs about magic. The Protestant churches also have different meanings in each region —so different, in some cases, that they amount to new religions. The purpose and conception of education held by authorities in the school system often vary greatly from the actual function and results in the schoolroom, where, for instance, the former requirement that teaching be in English was frequently frustrated by the fact that the teachers themselves often scarcely knew English. The formal platforms of political parties tend to be composites and compromises of the political ideologies of different classes and localities. The army is more than a military organization. Its racial practices have strongly furthered the Puerto Rico independence movement; its grants to veterans of World War II have put a large number of men in school and have financed business ventures for others, particularly a large and distinctive group of taxicab owners who now form an interesting and highly mobile, insular sociocultural subsegment; and for many individuals it is a means of escape from economic insecurity.

A great deal of community culture, in other words, consists of local manifestations of the more formal institutions, although some activities are strictly local and lack island-wide cohesion, organization, or even common features, except as they are part of the Puerto Rico culture area. This portion of culture consists largely of those matters in which the individual has some freedom of choice as contrasted with others in which his behavior is prescribed by the culture. Marriage, for instance, functions on a local and personal level insofar as there is freedom of choice within the limits of finance, class status, and other circumstances. A person may choose his spouse according to his class; he may have a church wedding or content himself with a consensual union. He may not, however, readily marry out of his social class because his social, economic, and political status are largely prescribed by wealth, occupation, locality, and even race.

These two aspects of insular institutions, the formal and the local, represent traditional division of labor among the social sciences and suggest terms of collaboration. The former are the concern of many specialists; the latter, in their community or class manifestations, are subjects for a cultural or social anthropological approach. The following two lists which are based on the Puerto Rican data illustrate how these aspects are distinctive and yet complementary:

Local aspects	Formal, insular institutions
Production, consumption, and trade	Insular economy, markets, etc.
Land tenure	Basic economy; land laws
Settlement pattern	No national institution
Family	No national institution
Social classes	Insular social structure
Occupational groups	Mobile labor; some unions
Local government	National government
Political affiliations and ideologies	National political parties
Local associations	National clubs and societies
Church and supernaturalism	Organized churches
Schools and learning	Educational system
Recreation	Organized sports (baseball)
Hospitals, doctors, curers	Government health measures

The totality of the local aspects of culture constitutes the way of life in each community or class but reveals little about the ultimate causes of change. In an area like Puerto Rico the principal sources of change clearly lie outside the area. It was postulated that Puerto Rican culture might be affected from the outside in two ways: first, through direct diffusion of culture; second, through changes in the basic institutions, which would penetrate in some way to every community, altering the local configurations and creating conditions that make diffusion a selective process. It is probable that very little cultural change is ever a simple mechanical process in which detached items are borrowed from elsewhere and added to the local inventory. The use of automobiles, for example, is not simply borrowed; it is a feature that depends upon economic status, social or business needs, and a complex of highways, servicing arrangements, mechanical skills, and other factors in a total situation. Similarly, labor unions do not appear merely because of cultural contacts. A union organizer from the outside can accomplish nothing unless a certain social, economic, and employment situation exists.

The more important factors in Puerto Rico's cultural change, therefore, appeared to penetrate the Island along axes of the basic institutions. To explain the contemporary culture, it was necessary to know what the earlier culture had been and to examine the effect of such formal institutions as: world markets in relation to land potentialities in an agrarian area; capitalization and credit facilities for reconversion of crops, mechanization, processing, shipping, and marketing; economic legislation that favored the Island as a dependency through allowing rebates and eliminating tariffs, and that handicapped it in relationship to other producers within the economic sphere of the United States by establishing quotas and other restrictions; social legislation that affected wages, hours, and conditions of employment; political institutions, within both Puerto Rico and the United States, that determined the formal means of providing economic and social legislation; the interaction of economic, social, and nationalistic forces which determine political power and the actual enactment of specific laws; the auxiliary roles of the church, education, philosophy, political ideologies, and various forms of propaganda in explaining the legislative decisions and the economic and social practices that are carried out within the limitations of these decisions.

These and many other problems of importance in understanding how the way of life in Puerto Rico as a whole and in the different communities have changed necessitate inquiries extending beyond Puerto Rico to the United States and farther, and special studies of the institutions or particular phenomena involved. In the corporate-owned sugar area, for example, the laboring class community, the special family structure, the strength of certain Protestant faiths, and other features have to be explained by environmental, legislative, economic, and other circumstances that favored the introduction of the basic pattern of land use.

In order to understand how insular and extra-insular institutions were causing changes in the Island and in its different regions, a series of conferences were arranged with specialists on the different subjects. Pertinent literature had already been examined, and lists of what seemed to be the more important questions were drawn up. The conferences consisted of all-day and sometimes two-day sessions with agronomists, rural sociologists, religious leaders, labor officials and leaders, economists, historians, political scientists, and other persons.

As the objective of studying the social anthropology of Puerto Rico meant in a practical sense that the project had to concentrate on the cultures of the Island's principal social segments, the information obtained from the specialists in other disciplines had to be used primarily in explaining the differences between and the changes in the groups studied. There are endless problems still to be studied in the other disciplines, but findings on each will further illuminate the problems of insular culture change. That is to say, most research will proceed along the usual disciplinary lines, but we think that our conceptualization of Puerto Rico as a sociocultural whole has made it theoretically and methodologically possible to relate the work of other disciplines to the problems of social anthropology.

This conceptualization also would make the findings of social anthropology important to the problems of the other disciplines. It would suggest that if the insular institutions are conceived as having local manifestations as well as formal aspects, many studies of the latter could utilize the data of community studies. A political movement, for example, has not only its national organization and ideology but its grass roots. The national ideology is a synthesis of the diversified local ideologies, and the latter are affected not only by political motivations but by social and economic factors and by religious beliefs. Political science and social anthropology could well cooperate on such a problem. Any formal institution, political, religious, or economic, has its grass roots where it flourishes or dies in the soil and climate of the total way of life of groups of individuals.

IMPLICATIONS FOR INTERDISCIPLINARY AREA RESEARCH

The Puerto Rico project does not pretend to and could not provide any final answer as to how the social science disciplines should be integrated in an area approach. It does show, however, how many problems stemming out of social anthropology require and may utilize data of other disciplines.

An ideal interdisciplinary analysis of the culture of Puerto Rico would include the following:
  I. Culture history
  II. Community studies
  III. Comparative studies
    1. Social organization of the Island
    2. Supernaturalism and the church
    3. Government and political ideologies
    4. Economics
    5. Socialization
  IV. Formal institutions
  V. Synthesis and hypotheses of possible cross-cultural validity

I. The culture history should cover, first, the development of the way of life as it is manifest in the localities and, second, the principal institutions as they are interrelated. The difficulty in getting the first task done is that the sources afford comparatively little material on community life. The second task is complicated by the historians' preoccupation with one or another special aspect of history, particularly military and political history, and by the inherent difficulty of describing all institutions as functional parts of a single area whole.

II. Community studies representing the greater part of the Island population have been made. They cover not only the contemporary way of life but trace changes since 1898, when Puerto Rico became a United States dependency, and attempt to show how the principal institutions have affected and are affecting each community. These community studies by no means exhaust the need for studies of sociocultural segments. Needlework, fishing, all-Negro, and other communities, though involving fewer people, should also be studied. The urban centers should be investigated with respect to their composition as well as the processes of urbanization. Moreover, many of the problems touched on in the project could be made the subject of more extended investigation, for example, race relations, total class structure, horizontal and vertical mobility, migration, and development of slums.

III. The comparative studies should include two kinds of material: (1) a statement of the variations of the local features arranged under the five general headings indicated, and (2) the relationship of these variations to the formal institutions. So far as the project's field data are concerned, it is fairly simple to show how marriage, the family, land use, land tenure, production, folk religion, local political attitudes, and the like vary from region to region and to interrelate them to one another within the local context. But many of these phenomena are local aspects of or are strongly affected by insular or larger institutions, and the latter are being studied by persons of several disciplines.

IV. An ideal area study would certainly include special sections on the formal insular-wide or larger institutions—government, legislation, commerce, banking, industry, churches, education, and others—which would be interrelated, the terms of reference being provided by such general themes as power structure, economic development, changing social structure, external relations, and political ideologies. In Puerto Rico research on these subjects is being carried on by many persons, and we could do no more than consult these persons and their writings in order to understand better the regional variations of community culture which constituted the objective of the study.

V. An "area discipline" would presumably be an approach which interrelates studies of culture history, sociocultural segments, variations in local manifestations of formal institutions, and insular-wide formal institutions in a single grand synthesis. Such a synthesis is now inconceivable. General interpretations of Puerto Rico in the future as in the past will no doubt spring from special interests and points of view, such as political history, colonialism, nationalistic ideology, economic dependency, and standards of living.

The Puerto Rico report did not aspire or presume to subsume all special interests, points of view, and problems in a single master interpretation. Instead, it endeavored to formulate certain hypotheses as causal explanations of cultural function and change in the communities studied which may obtain also in other areas where the same conditions are found. The hypotheses necessarily include the data of all social sciences, even though they pertain to interests that develop principally in the study of rural peoples, for example, land use, land tenure, social structure, political features, and religion. They can be tested by research in other world areas, subareas, and regions, the general being abstracted from the particulars of the local cultural tradition in each case. This procedure, we believe, is essential if social science is to have true predictive value. The future trends of Puerto Rico will be understandable only if a knowledge of basic cross-culturally validated cause and effect is combined with a knowledge of what is specific to the Hispanic heritage.

CHAPTER V

SUMMARY AND CONCLUSIONS

This bulletin undertook an analysis of social science theory and method which may be developed in an interdisciplinary area approach. It is recognized, of course, that area studies may have purposes and methods other than those with which we are concerned here. It is undeniable, however, that these studies more than almost any previous research squarely pose the question of how the data of the various social sciences and humanities can be interrelated in terms of a whole which is more than the sum of its parts. Area studies are not the only kind of interdisciplinary approach but at present they are one of the most important. There is little doubt that if the nature of the interrelationship of area phenomena can be adequately conceptualized, research problems clearly stated, and appropriate methods developed, we shall not only further social science theory but clarify many practical problems of human relations, which in the last analysis are the reasons for research.

The compelling necessity to know as much as possible about the major world areas, especially about the behavior of people in these areas, has led to the assembling of a considerable variety of specialists in area study centers. Initially it is to be expected that each expert would contribute to knowledge according to the traditional concepts and methods of his discipline. Association of scholars, especially in interdisciplinary research seminars and projects, will gradually affect the thinking of each participant. Accomplishments of this kind are, however, beyond the scope of this bulletin; only participants could adequately describe the effects of cross-fertilization brought about through frequent personal meetings and exchange of ideas.

Another means of achieving interdisciplinary integration in

SUMMARY AND CONCLUSIONS

area research is through planned projects which conceptualize area, formulate problems, and devise methods in such a way that teamwork is required and the data of the different disciplines are truly interrelated. This procedure faces the difficulty that an area discipline does not now exist and that any formulation of problems and methods may bear the stamp of the special training of the planner. Experience has shown, however, that joint research projects can be planned so as to interest and attract a variety of personnel. This is particularly true when the research is devoted to some central problem, such as the study of nationalism, foreign relations, effects of industrialization, or regional contrasts. These general interests or themes tend to lack a disciplinary stamp and they orient a great deal of research that is not closely planned as a single project (see pp. 3–4, 83–94); and in the writer's opinion it may be safely predicted that many more planned projects in the future will find these themes broken down into a series of fairly concrete problems, each of which will guide the research of participating disciplines.

The concrete formulation of any research problem and the particular interrelationship of relevant data are determined, however, by the characteristics of a given area. This raises the question whether it is possible to conceptualize area in such a way that it will serve all interdisciplinary area research. Area phenomena are interrelated in the context of a structured whole. The characteristics of the whole—the patterns of economic, social, religious, political, esthetic, and other special aspects of behavior—are determined by cultural heritage, but they are interrelated within the framework of particular societies. The unit of area study therefore must be a sociocultural whole or system.

The concept of the sociocultural whole would seem to be essential to any interdisciplinary area research. The concept of the culture area has limited value, for it is based on regularities that occur among different societies in a particular area.

The heterogeneous institutions and behavior patterns of any culture have a functional interdependence and reciprocity only within particular societies. As the institutions and special patterns of behavior constitute the subject matter of different disciplines, particularly in the more complex societies, the concept of the sociocultural system is the only conceivable frame of reference for interdisciplinary area research.

The concept of the sociocultural system does not of itself constitute a guide for any area research. It is simply an elucidation of the idea that area phenomena are interrelated in some sort of coherent way. Each area has its distinctive tradition and organization, which is expressed by the concept of cultural relativity. Moreover, within the cultural tradition of each area, sociocultural systems have developed through a succession of levels, each higher level being not only more complex than the lower but qualitatively different in that it has characteristics that were not evident in antecedent patterns. Finally, each sociocultural system has become increasingly linked with other systems. Area research problems and methods therefore must be adapted to the society's unique cultural patterns, to its level of development or organization, and to its dependency relations with other societies. In short, the phenomena studied by the different disciplines must be interrelated within the context of a whole which has a sufficient degree of structural and functional unity to have some cohesion, but the problems investigated and the methods will vary considerably according to the nature of the sociocultural system.

Small independent sociocultural wholes, such as tribal societies, are currently studied in their entirety by anthropology alone. In more complex systems of higher levels, the ethnographic approach of anthropology may be used to obtain a qualitative picture of the culture of communities, classes, ethnic groups, races, or other special segments and divisions of the whole. But these segments cannot be approached as if they were self-contained tribal societies. They must be studied in

SUMMARY AND CONCLUSIONS 153

terms of their relationship to one another and to the formal institutions found throughout the total sociocultural system. A unidisciplinary approach is inadequate.

The traditional approach to the large and complex sociocultural systems found in the contemporary world has been through special disciplines—geography, economics, sociology, political science, history, philosophy, linguistics, etc. The inadequacy of excessive compartmentalization of knowledge has become very apparent when traditional methods, developed largely in the study of Euro-American industrialized societies, have been applied to other world areas. The problem of interrelating the findings of all disciplines in terms of some kind of totality of knowledge of each world area is not yet solved. Meanwhile, the most fruitful means of integrating area data is to relate them to basic problems which may develop out of one or another interest or discipline.

Scientific area study is not content with mere analytic description of phenomena which distinguish areas. It seeks to generalize knowledge and to find laws of human behavior. This approach to area study is at present largely implicit in the fact that certain broad interests are evident in the research on different areas. But a scientific methodology leading to generalization has not been made explicit. Too often the developmental processes and functional interrelationships of phenomena observed in one area are regarded as universal human characteristics, although the hypotheses involved have not been systematically tested in other areas. There is needed a more explicit methodology which, as suggested in preceding pages, should include the following procedures: (1) A theme of interest, for example, the development of nationalism, may be reduced to a concrete problem. Hunches about nationalism may be converted into hypotheses concerning the conditions which give rise to nationalism. (2) An area analysis should relate nationalism to the total sociocultural system, a task requiring the cooperation of many disciplines. The validity of the initial hypothesis can be tested only by such total area analysis, for otherwise it would be impossible to know which manifestations of nationalism were the product of unique characteristics of the area and which resulted from regularities of cause and effect that are found in several different areas. (3) The specific conditions which give rise to nationalism should be reformulated or restated as hypotheses which can be tested in other areas. This in turn requires that sociocultural systems be classified by an empirical method, the conditions involved in each hypothesis serving as taxonomic criteria.

The problem approach thus has two great values to area studies. First, it provides terms for the cooperation of several disciplines by defining and delimiting the scope of investigation. An analytic study of a total area is too broad and diffuse to be manageable. Study of a special problem is concrete and feasible. Second, it makes possible the construction of hypotheses concerning basic patterns of human behavior. It is a step toward generalizing knowledge about human beings in that it seeks specific, delimited, and testable hypotheses rather than vague universal laws.

The concepts and methods set forth here were illustrated by the Puerto Rico project. The broad problem was to ascertain how the influences emanating from a highly industrialized society affected the local or regional varieties of culture found in one of its agrarian dependencies. The breakdown into concrete hypotheses was determined by the characteristics of the two societies—one an industrialized, continental, political democracy and the other an agrarian subtropical island, which had been a colony of Spain and had become a dependency of the United States. It was presumed that, despite certain distinctive characteristics of each society, the political, economic, and general cultural influences of the United States on Puerto Rico would follow certain patterns which were manifest elsewhere in the world under similar conditions.

As the Island is quite heterogeneous in environment, a

SUMMARY AND CONCLUSIONS 155

method of cultural ecology was used to explain the principal local variations in culture. Influences first from Spain and later from the United States were potentially available to the entire Island, but actually the local differences in environment entailed different types of land use which in turn caused sharp variations in the cultures of the different communities. Communities in the corporate-owned sugar region, the government-owned sugar region, the coffee region, and the mixed crop region represent quite unlike ways of life.

To understand the influences that have been changing these communities, it was necessary to understand the insular-wide economic, political, legal, religious, and other institutions, including changes in the latter under United States sovereignty. This required frequent consultation with specialists on these institutions. The cultural processes which brought about both insular-wide features and local differences in Puerto Rico were formulated as hypotheses that can be tested elsewhere under like conditions.

The ultimate justification of social science research is that it can predict trends in human affairs—that it can state with some precision what will take place under specifiable circumstances. If sociocultural levels represent qualitatively new kinds of wholes, there may be theoretical reason for doubting whether social science can predict very far in advance what novel and as yet unknown sociocultural types will emerge. In most of the world, however, changes seem to run familiar courses: nonindustrial nations are becoming industrialized; people who had depended upon subsistence farming are being drawn into the orbit of a single economic world through conversion to cash crops or other produce and dependence upon industrially manufactured goods; local autonomy is yielding to national or foreign domination; economic and political dependency has recently been accompanied by a resurgence of nationalistic or culturalistic movements; ideological and religious systems implement such movements; social structure is being transformed; racial and ethnic relations acquire distinctive characteristics. Accompanying these and other changes are modifications in all parts of sociocultural systems.

These world-wide trends have distinctive local characteristics which are determined by the particular cultural tradition of each area; they may be seen in terms of cultural relativity. But they also have a great deal in common. By proper cross-cultural comparison it should be possible to formulate recurrent regularities in developmental processes and functional relationships. These regularities will rarely be universal social science laws. Instead, they will be hypotheses or formulations of cultural and social change which can be expected under precisely stipulated conditions. They may pertain to sociocultural systems of varying sizes and degrees of complexity or to special institutions and combinations of institutions. In an interdisciplinary approach to any area they will represent conclusions which are so presented as to constitute a problem or hypothesis for research in other areas which have somewhat similar sociocultural systems. If the formulations develop from major themes of interest, they will require the data of many different disciplines.

INDEX OF NAMES

Allen, F. L., 73
Arensberg, C. M., 39, 44, 50, 123, 133, 134
Armstrong, R., 128n
Ashton, J. W., xvi

Bateson, G., 80
Beals, R. L., xvi, 12, 28, 34, 58, 59n, 60, 61, 63
Beard, C. A., 77
Beard, M. R., 77
Bell, E. H., 41n
Benedict, R., 80, 82, 99n
Bennett, W. C., xvi, 36, 38n
Bird, J., 36
Bishop, C. W., 77
Blegen, T. C., xvi
Brand, D. D., 58, 60n, 61
Brown, W. N., xvi, 11n, 17n, 100
Bryce, J., 73
Buck, J. L., 119
Buitrón, A., 32n, 57n
Burgess, E. W., 93

Cárdenas, L., 58
Caro, I., 128n
Carrasco, P., 34n, 59n, 63–64
Cayton, H. R., 27, 40
Chang, C., 27n, 119
Chen, T., 50
Collier, D., 36
Collier, J., Jr., xi, 32n, 57n
Cottrell, L. S., Jr., xvi
Creel, H. G., 77

Davis, A., 27, 40
Davis, K., 131
Dollard, J., 27, 40
Dos Passos, J., 73
Drake, St. C., 27, 40
Du Bois, C., xvi, 80

Eggan, F., xvi
Embree, J. F., xvi, 18, 29n, 38, 40, 50, 78, 82, 133

Escobar, G., 35
Evans, C., 36

Fainsod, M., 90
Fairbank, J. K., 73–75, 79, 86, 105
Fei, H., 26–27, 29n, 38n, 52, 119, 133
Fenton, W. N., xiin
Fisher, H. H., xvi
Forde, J., 36
Foster, G. M., Jr., 29n, 58, 60–61

Gardner, B. B., 27, 40
Gardner, M. R., 27, 40
Gillin, J., 28, 34–35, 55, 56, 57
Gorer, G., 80, 81
Gunther, J., 73
Gustafson, A., xvi

Hall, R. B., vii, xiin, xvi, 5, 14n, 15–16
Hallowell, A. I., 80
Haring, D. G., 75n, 76, 79, 80
Hatt, P., 131
Herodotus, 73
Herring, P., xvi, 95
Herskovits, M. J., 30n
Hicks, G., 31
Hilton, R., xvi
Holmberg, A., 36–37
Hsu, F. L. K., 26, 27, 28, 38, 52, 75n, 76, 79
Humboldt, von, A., 73

James, P., xvii
Joseph, A., 42

Kardiner, A., 80
Keesing, F. M., xvii
Kidder, A. V., xi, xvii, 118
Kimball, S. T., 39, 44, 50, 123, 133, 134
Klineberg, O., 80n
Kluckhohn, C., xvii, 16n, 80
Kollmorgen, W. M., 41n
Kubler, G., 38n

LaFarge, O., 38n
Latourette, K. S., 77
Lattimore, O., xvii, 19, 52, 86, 87
Laufer, B., 77
Leonard, I. A., xiin
Leonard, O., 29n, 41n, 42
Lewis, S., 117
Linton, R., 30n, 41n, 56n, 75n, 80
Loomis, C. P., 29n, 41n, 42
Low, J. O., 39n
Lowie, R. H., 78
Lunt, P. S., 27n, 39n
Lynd, H. M., 23, 26, 28, 30–31, 50, 133
Lynd, R., 23, 26, 28, 30–31, 50, 133

Malinowski, B., 99n
Manners, R., 128n
Marco Polo, 73
McBryde, F. W., 36–37
McCorkle, T., 34n, 59n
McKenzie, R. D., 93
MacLeish, K., 41n
Mead, M., 30, 78, 80
Mintz, S., 128n
Mishkin, B., 38n
Moe, E. O., 41n
More, Sir Thomas, 58
Morgan, L. H., 113
Muelle, J., 35, 37
Murra, J., 128n
Murray, H. A., 80n

Northrop, F. S. C., 95n
Novikoff, A. B., 109n

Odum, H. W., xvii, 54n, 57, 66–68, 93, 94
Ortega, D., 128n
Ospina, G., 60n

Padilla, E., 128n
Park, R. E., 93
Parsons, E. C., 26, 28, 32, 33, 35, 46, 56, 57, 61
Parsons, T., 67, 95
Perkins, D., 74n

Pico, R., 128
Pierson, D., 41n
Powdermaker, H., 27, 40, 47

Quiroga, Bishop, 58

Radcliffe-Brown, A. R., 99n
Redfield, R., 26, 30n, 33, 35, 61, 93, 111, 113, 133
Robinson, G. T., xvii
Roca, A., 128n
Rogler, C. C., 128
Rosario, C., 128n
Rottenberg, S., 127n
Rowe, J. H., 38n
Rubin de la Borbolla, D. F., 58, 59n

Sansom, G. B., 77
Scheele, R., 128n
Seda, E., 128n
Senior, C., 127n
Shadick, H., xvii
Siegel, M., 128, 134
Smedley, A., 86
Smith, T. L., xvii, 77
Snow, E., 86
Somervell, D. C., 104n
Sorokin, P. A., 95n, 106n, 112
Spengler, O., 104
Srole, L., 39n
Steward, J. H., vii, viii, 38n, 65n, 103n, 112n, 119n, 120n
Strong, W. D., 36
Sumner, W. G., 107

Tannenbaum, F., 41n, 131
Taylor, C. C., 27, 41n
Taylor, G. E., xvii
Thompson, L., 42
Thorner, A., 75n
Thorner, D., 75n, 76
Toynbee, A. J., 104
Tschopik, H., Jr., 34–35, 36, 56

Wagley, C., viii, xiin, xvii, 12n, 60n, 79 96n

INDEX

Ware, C., 128
Warner, W. L., 27, 31, 39n, 46-47, 49
Wauchope, R., xvii, 94
Webbink, P., xvii
Welles, S., 74
West, J., 23, 26, 31
West, R. C., 58, 60n, 61
Whetten, N. L., 77
Whitaker, A. P., 74n
Willey, G. R., 36

Wilson, M. L., xi
Wissler, C., 9n, 23, 24
Wittfogel, K. A., 77, 113
Wolf, E., 128n
Wright, W. L., xvii
Wynne, W., 40n, 41n

Yang, M. C., 26, 27, 38, 52
Young, K., 41n

Zimmerman, C. C., 54n

INDEX OF SUBJECTS

Abstraction, 97, 100, 113-114, 120-122, 149
Acculturation, 30, 32-34, 38n, 42, 43, 44, 48, 78, 79, 94
Afghanistan, 10
Africa, 9
Agraristas, 64
Agriculture, 37, 39, 41, 43, 48, 69, 91, 123-124, 135
American Council of Learned Societies, xi
American Museum of Natural History, 36
Amish, 42, 43, 105
Andes, 32, 44, 67, 103
Architecture, 36
Area: concept of, 1; criteria of, 67-68; definition of, 7; discipline, xv-xvi, 16; unit, nature of, xv, 8-13, 56-57, 126, 151; "whole," xvi, 2, 50, 51, 55, 62, 65, 66-67, 68, 84, 95-96, 99-100, 106, 126, 127, 128-129, 133, 137, 140-147, 151
Armed services, xii, 143
Asia, 92; Central, 11, 19; East, 86; South, 9, 11, 100; Southeast, 9, 11, 15, 17, 100; see also Department of South Asia Regional Studies
Attitudes, 40-41, 47, 81, 82, 94, 130, 137, 140, see also Behavior

Bands, patrilineal, 112, 120
Baseball, 101-102, 103
Behavior, patterns of, 6, 35, 56, 68, 70, 78, 80-81, 82, 97-98, 99, 108, 118, 150, 152, 153-154
Biological analogy, 96, 109-110
Brazil, 9, 33, 77, 79, see also Institute for Brazilian Studies

California, University of, 34, 57-58
Carnegie Corporation of New York, xii
Carnegie Institution of Washington, xi, 33, 118
Case histories, 45, 139
Caste, 40
Catholicism, 49, 56, 58, 64, 142
Cause and effect, 118, 120-125, 149, 154
Center for Japanese Studies, University of Michigan, 15, 17
Centers, area study, xi, xii, 18, 150
Ceramics, 36, 64
Ceylon, 10
Cherán, 60
Chicago, 40
Chicago Natural History Museum, 36
Chicago, University of, 128n, 131
China, 9, 14n, 15, 19, 26-27, 28, 38, 50, 52-53, 73-74, 75-76, 77, 79, 81, 84, 86, 89, 103, 105, 119
Civilization, vs. nation, 102-104, 113

Clan, 112
Class, 27, 31, 39-40, 44, 46, 49, 56, 65, 68, 70-71, 81, 87, 89, 116-117, 121, 133, 137, 138-139, 140, 141-142, 143, 145
Collectivization, 37, 52-53
Colombia, 33
Columbia University, xiv, 3, 14, 15, 17, 31, 36, 63, 121, 128n, 130-131
Communism: Chinese, 52-53, 74, 105; Russian, 16, 52, 90-91, 105
Community studies, 20-53, 58, 60, 65, 67, 70, 93, 105, 107, 115-116, 128, 131, 132, 133-139, 148
Competition, 68, 101-104
Context, of larger society, 22-24, 31, 32, 38, 43, 49-50, 51, 55, 57, 62-64, 65, 70-71, 110, 115, 129, 132, 148, 152
Creole, 55-56
Cross-cultural research, 5-6, 19, 21, 68-69, 112, 113, 117-125, 149, 156
Cross-fertilization, 8, 15-17, 150
Cultural relativity, 2, 4, 5, 69, 107, 117, 152, 156
"Cultural shock," 4
Culture: area, 7, 9-12, 54-56, 57, 61, 66, 70, 78, 99-102, 106, 121, 140, 143, 151; carrier, 97; complex, 99, 108; concept of, 1, 97-106, 117; conservatism, 42, 43, 60; contact, 133-134, 141, 145; content, 55-57, 61; definition of, 98; deviants, 42, 43, 48; differences, 41, 48-49, 116-117, 133; diffusion, 144; ecology, 110, 120, 133, 136, 155; elements, 46, 47, 55, 62, 99-100, 107-108; factors, 81, 82, 94; history, 37, 68, 99, 102, 104, 130, 140, 147, 149; national, 67, 77, 79, 81, 111; patterns of, 4, 42, 45, 55, 78, 80-81, 99-100, 103-105, 107, 108, 131, 152; and personality, 26-27, 31, 38, 42-43, 78, 80-81, 97-98, 106; process, 35, 37, 136, 155; trends, 102, 118, 138; types, 34, 35, see also Taxonomy; see also Culture change, Folk culture, Hispanic influences, Indian elements, Society, Stability

Culture change, 25, 37, 38n, 40, 43, 48-49, 51, 59, 65, 92, 98, 101-106, 110, 144-146, 149, 156

Definitions, 6-8
Demographic trends, see Population
Departamento Autónomo de Asuntas Indígenas, 57
Department of South Asia Regional Studies, University of Pennsylvania, 10, 15-16
Depression, 31

Economic factors, 6, 26, 38, 39, 41, 42, 52, 59, 61, 63, 87, 91, 123-124, 130-131, 146, 147, 155
Ecuador, 26, 32, 46, 56-57, 93
Education, 48, 69, 142-143
Egypt, 103
Empires, 53, 102-104
England, 84
Environment, 10, 59, 98, 113, 133, 141, 146, 154, 155
Escuela Nacional de Antropología, 57, 58, 63
Ethnic groups, see Minorities
Ethnocentrism, 4, 45, 130
Ethnographic method, 21-39, 40, 41, 43, 45-46, 47, 55, 60-62, 79, 83, 115, 116, 139, 143-144, 152
Europe: Central, 9; Eastern, 9, 10, 14, 17; Western, 9, 104
European Institute, Columbia University, 15

Family, 38, 39, 48, 110, 112, 121, 145
Far East, 9, 11, 14n, 88, 89
Far Eastern Institute, University of Washington, 14n
Field techniques, 44-47, 59, 63, 67, 131, 135, 139
Folk culture, 26, 32-35, 62, 64, 65, 67-68, 70, 71, 93, 107, 111, 116, 127, 131
Folk society, 26, 34, 35, 62, 65, 68, 71, 107, 111-113, 127, 140
Foreign relations, see International relations

INDEX

Geographic criteria, 9, 10, 11, 12, 54, 68, 96, 127
Geographic research, 9, 13, 36, 37, 58, 60
Germany, 78, 81, 105

Harvard University, 14, 15, 16, 73, 74, 90
Health, 85–86
Hispanic influences, in culture, 11–12, 26, 32–35, 44, 46, 55–57, 62, 64, 65, 66, 70, 107, 121, 129, 131–132, 133, 136, 138, 140, 149, 155
Historical method, 21, 24–25, 30, 32, 37, 38, 39, 40, 41, 51, 61, 64, 79, 102, 108, 130, 140
Hopi, 42–43
Hypotheses: formulation of, 119–124, 149, 154, 156; testing of, 45, 124–125, 149, 153–154, 155

Ideologies, 44, 53, 63, 65, 78, 82, 83, 87, 88, 89–91, 105, 143, 146, 155, *see also* Values
India, 10, 17, 19, 75–76, 81, 84, 89, 100, 103
Indian (American) elements, in culture, 26, 32–35, 44, 46, 55–56, 57, 62, 65, 107
Indiana, 33
Indiana University, 10, 14, 17
Indians: Andean, 32; Central American, 32; North American, xi, 30; Pueblo, 32; *see also* Hopi, Latin America, Maya, Tarascan Indians
Indonesian Republic, 100
Industrial revolution, 104
Industrialization, 24, 37, 53, 69, 70, 71, 89, 154, 155
Insights, 24, 28, 31, 32, 130, 131
Institute for Brazilian Studies, Vanderbilt University, 15
Institute of Andean Research, 36
Institutions, social, 0, 48, 50, 63, 64, 65–66, 68, 70–71, 72, 77, 78, 79, 106, 108, 115–117, 126, 127, 128n, 129, 130, 140–147, 148, 149, 152, 153, 155, 156

Instituto de Antropología é Historia, 63
Integration: area, 1, 15–19, 33, 61, 62, 63, 69, 73, 84, 126, 153; concepts, 95–106; of culture, 43, 62, 63, 65, 70, 83, 100, 137; definition of, 95; levels of, 106–114; of personality, 43, 80, 97–98; of social science, 2, 69, 72, 73, 83, 95, 114, 117, 129, 147, 150
Interaction, 101
Interdisciplinary cooperation, xii, 2, 4, 7, 12, 13–19, 20, 37, 66, 68, 72, 83, 86, 96, 126, 127, 153, 154
Interdisciplinary research, xi, xiii, xv, 1, 5, 8, 13, 15, 34, 57, 58, 69, 70, 72, 73, 85, 87, 93, 109, 117, 126, 141, 147–149, 150, 151, 152, 156; vs. multidisciplinary, xv, 7–8, 18, 69–70
International relations, xiii, 3, 7, 72, 74–75, 79, 86–87
Interview, 24, 45, 139
Iran, 19
Ireland, 39, 44, 50, 123, 134
Isolation, 43, 59, 62
Italy, 105

Japan, 9, 17, 38, 40, 50, 75–76, 77, 78, 79, 81, 82, 89, 104, 105, *see also* Center for Japanese Studies
Johns Hopkins University, 13, 19
Joint Committee on Latin American Studies, xii

Kinship, 39, 56, 111, 112

Land ownership, 123, 135, 138
Land tenure, 52–53, 91, 119, 140
Land use, 53, 60, 65, 91, 113, 119, 135, 141, 146, 155
Language, 10, 14, 24, 32, 130, 140
Latin America, xi, xii, xiv, 9, 11, 14n, 15, 17, 31–33, 37, 55–56, 77, 121–122, 131, 140
Laws, general, *see* Universals
"Life cycle," 26, 28, 31, 38

Marriage, 143

Maya, xi, 33, 110, 118
Mesopotamia, 103
Mestizos, 35, 56, 60–61
Methods: comparative, 1, 21, 25–29, 37, 38, 39, 40, 41, 42, 51, 66, 70, 83, 90, 108, 112, 114, 128n, 148; qualititative, 22, 43, 45, 46, 47, 48, 49, 67, 135, 139–140, 152; quantitative, 22, 39, 43, 45–49, 66, 67, 116, 134, 135, 139–140; *see also* Ethnographic method, Historical method
Mexico, xi, 12, 26, 28, 32, 33–34, 56, 57, 58, 61, 62, 64, 65, 77, 93
Michigan, University of, 15, 17
Middle America, 9, 32, 94, 103
Middle American Research Institute, Tulane University, 12, 94
Minnesota, University of, 10, 15, 16
Minorities, 39, 44, 78, 89, 94
Mississippi, 40
Missouri, 31
Mitla, 32, 61
Moche, 34–35, 56, 57, 93
Mongolia, Inner, 9

Nation, 71, 112, 113
"National character," 78, 80–83, 97
National Research Council, xi–xii; Committee on Asian Anthropology, 82, 88, 90, 92
National structure, 87, 88–89, 94
National studies, 71–83, 91
Nationalism, 19, 53, 74, 79, 84, 87–88, 100, 105, 153–154, 155
Near East, 9, 10, 11, 103, 104
Negro, American, 40, 41, 47
Nepal, 10
North Carolina, 69
North Carolina, University of, 57, 69
Northwestern University, 14n

Objectives, of area research, 1–6, 68, 84

Pacific-Asiatic program, Stanford University, 15
Pacific Islands, 9

Pakistan, 10, 17, 75–76
Pan-Islam, 10, 11, 84
Participant observation, 31, 45, 139
Peguche, 32, 46, 57, 93
Pennsylvania, 42, 105
Pennsylvania, University of, 10–11, 15, 16
Personality, 43, 80, 81, 83, 97–98
Personnel, 13, 14, 17–19, 63, 128n, 150, 151
Peru, 28, 33, 34–37, 44, 56–57, 93, 107–108
Piedmont, 69
Population, 40, 41, 42, 69, 92
Power, 53, 105, 121, 139
Prediction, xiii, 117–118, 137, 149, 155
Prejudice, 41
Princeton University, 10
"Problem" approach, xv, 18–19, 25–26, 66, 68–69, 83–94, 112, 117–125, 133, 151, 153, 154, 156
Proletarianization, 35
Psychological factors, 40, 42, 80–81, 83, 94, 97–98, 108, 110
Psychological tests, 43
Puerto Rico, xiv, xvi, 44, 49, 65, 66, 67, 81, 121–123, 126–149, 154
Puerto Rico, University of, 127–128n, 131

Quechua, 34, 35
Questionnaire, 45, 46, 49, 67, 116, 119, 139
Quiroga, 61

Race relations, 27, 40–41, 44, 68, 94, 140, 143, 155–156
Reductionism, 109
Regionalism, 63, 66, 67, 68, 134, 135, 137, 149, 154
Regions, 54–71, 94, 155
Religion, 63–64, 142, 145, *see also* Catholicism
Research planning, 8, 17–19, 58, 84, 117, 151
Resettlement, xi, 92, 138

INDEX

Rockefeller Foundation, 128n
Rural Life Studies, 27, 40, 41-42, 50
Russia, 3-4, 9, 10, 14n, 15, 16, 17, 19, 86, 90-91, 105
Russian Institute, Columbia University, 3, 14, 17
Russian Research Center, Harvard Unicersity, 14, 16, 90

Sampling, 34, 37, 39, 44-47, 67, 139
Scandinavia, 9, 10, 15, 16
Sectionalism, 68
Seminars, area, 8, 15-17, 131, 150
Seriation studies, 36, 64
Settlement, 36, 64, see also Resettlement
Sicaya, 35, 93
Sinarquistas, 64
Sinkiang, 19
Smithsonian Institution: Institute of Social Anthropology, xiv, 33-37, 44, 58, 63; War Background Studies, 78
Social change, 83, 89, 101-106, 110, 156
Social relations studies, 27, 39-43, 105
Social Science Research Center, University of Puerto Rico, 127n
Social Science Research Council, xii, 95
Society, 97-106
Sociocultural levels, 107-114, 115, 120, 121, 127, 152, 155
Sociocultural segments, 22, 51, 78, 93, 106, 115-116, 126, 130, 137, 138, 140, 141, 146, 148, 149, 152
Sociocultural whole, or system, 2, 4-5, 21, 22, 45, 50, 51, 55, 56-57, 62, 66, 67, 68, 70, 78, 88, 95, 99-100, 106-117, 124, 126, 127, 129, 140, 141, 146, 151-153, 154, 155, 156, see also Area whole
Southeastern United States, 57, 66-69, 70-71, 94
Sovereignty, 71-72
Spanish Conquest, 38, 62, 65, 110-111
Stability: community, 27, 40, 41-43, 44, 50, 105; cultural, 42, 105
Stanford University, 11, 13, 15, 17
Status, 39, 40, 56, 82, 143

Stratigraphic studies, 36, 64
Structural-functional relationships, 10, 54, 55, 67, 70, 106-114, 115, 120-121, 126, 127-128, 152, 153, 156
Supernaturalism, 111
Survey, see Field techniques
"Survivals," 107, 136, 138

Tarascan Indians, xi, 12, 33-34, 57-66, 70-71, 93, 116
Taxonomy (social), 112-114, 120-125
Technological factors, 24, 30, 68, 111
Tepotzlán, 61
Themes, of interest, xv, 3-4, 19, 45, 51, 53, 69, 72, 73, 74, 84-94, 114, 117, 148, 151, 153, 156
Training area, xi, xii, xiii, 7, 9, 130
Tribes, 1, 10, 21, 22, 25, 30, 37, 50, 54-55, 56, 59, 77, 79, 99, 112, 132, 152
Tulane University, 12, 94
Tzintzuntzan, 60, 61

United States, xii, 3, 5, 9, 45, 72, 73, 74, 75, 77, 78, 86, 116, 129
U. S. Agricultural Adjustment Administration, 135
U. S. Bureau of Agricultural Economics, 27, 41
U. S. Bureau of American Ethnology, 36
U. S. Bureau of the Census, 135
U. S. Bureau of Indian Affairs, xi, 30
U. S. Department of Agriculture, xi
U. S. Department of State, 33, 73
U. S. Federal Communications Commission, 76
U. S. Navy Department, 73
U. S. Office of Strategic Services, 73, 82
U. S. Office of War Information, 73
U. S. Soil Conservation Service, xi, 30
U. S. War Department, 73
"Universal pattern," 23, 24
"Universals," 5-6, 68, 69, 113, 118-120, 125, 153, 154, 156

Urbanization, 26, 33, 35, 44, 69, 92–93, 137, 140, 148
Utility, practical, of area research, xii–xiii, 2–4, 73, 85–86

Values, 83, 87, 89–91, 111, 130
Vanderbilt University, 15
Virginia, 69
Viru Valley, 36, 37, 64

Washington, University of, 14n
Wholes, see Area whole, Sociocultural whole
Wisconsin, University of, 10, 15
World War II, xi, xii–xiii, 2, 3, 78

Yale University, 11, 14n, 15, 17, 36
Yucatan, 26, 33, 93, 110–111, 113